BEHOLD

A MODERN LOOK AT THE BOOK OF REVELATION

Tina Ketch

BEHOLD
A MODERN LOOK AT THE BOOK OF REVELATION

ISBN: 979-8-9921669-2-7
eISBN: 979-8-9921669-3-4

PREFACE

For centuries, the Book of Revelation has fascinated, inspired, and often perplexed its readers. Its vivid imagery, powerful symbolism, and apocalyptic tone have led to countless interpretations, many of which focus on fear, judgment, and the end of the world. Yet, as I delved deeper into this sacred text, I discovered a different story—a story not of despair but of profound hope, renewal, and divine love.

Revelation is more than a prophecy about the future; it is a timeless message for our lives today. It invites us to reflect on our relationship with the divine, with one another, and with the world around us. It calls us to let go of fear and to embrace the transformative power of grace. Far from being a tale of destruction, Revelation is a roadmap to renewal, a guide to living with courage, compassion, and faith in the face of life's challenges.

This book was born from a desire to make Revelation accessible and meaningful for modern readers. It is not an attempt to decode every symbol or predict specific events but rather to explore the timeless truths that Revelation offers. Through its dramatic imagery—the seals, trumpets, bowls, the New Jerusalem, and more—Revelation speaks to the universal struggles and aspirations of humanity. It reminds us that even in the darkest moments, light prevails, and that every ending carries the promise of a new beginning.

Writing this book has been a journey of reflection and growth. It has deepened my understanding of the divine and my appreciation for the resilience of the human spirit. My hope is that it will do the same for you. Whether you approach Revelation with curiosity, skepticism, or faith, this book is an invitation to explore its message with an open heart and mind.

We live in a time that often feels tumultuous—marked by division, uncertainty, and rapid change. Yet, as Revelation reminds us, these moments of disruption can also be moments of transformation. They challenge us to let go of what no longer serves us and to build a world rooted in love, justice, and unity. Revelation is not a story about the end; it is a story about renewal. It is a call to action, urging us to participate in the divine work of healing and restoration.

I dedicate this book to all who seek hope in uncertain times, to those longing for clarity in a world of chaos, and to everyone striving to live with purpose and grace. May it inspire you to reflect, grow, and embrace the promise of renewal that Revelation offers.

With gratitude and hope,
Tina Ketch

TABLE OF CONTENTS

INTRODUCTION

UNLOCKING THE MYSTERY AND MESSAGE OF REVELATION

The Book of Revelation is, without question, one of the most intriguing and profound texts in the Bible. Its vivid imagery and layered symbolism have sparked centuries of reflection, debate, and wonder. A text filled with dragons and trumpets, seals and bowls, thrones and scrolls, Revelation captures the imagination like no other. Yet, for many, its message remains elusive. It has been read as a cryptic prophecy, a warning of apocalyptic doom, or an account of divine judgment. Its dramatic tone and enigmatic visions often evoke fear and confusion rather than understanding and hope.

But Revelation's true purpose is not to terrify or alienate—it is to inspire and transform. Beneath its striking imagery lies a timeless and deeply spiritual message: the promise of renewal, the assurance of divine grace, and the call to overcome life's challenges with courage and faith. To fully appreciate this message, we must approach Revelation not with dread but with openness, not with a desire to decode its mysteries, but with a willingness to embrace its truths.

THE MAN BEHIND THE VISION: JOHN OF PATMOS

To understand Revelation's profound message, it is essential to consider the context in which it was written and the life of its mysterious author, John of Patmos. Introduced simply as "John" in the opening verses, this figure identifies himself as a servant of Christ exiled on the rocky island of Patmos for his testimony of faith (Revelation 1:9). While the specifics of his identity remain a subject of debate, his role as the recipient and recorder of these apocalyptic visions is unquestionable.

Traditionally, John of Patmos has been identified with the Apostle John—the beloved disciple of Jesus and the author of the Gospel of John and the three Johannine epistles. Early Christian writers like

Justin Martyr and Irenaeus supported this connection, describing him as an elder statesman of faith who spent his later years guiding the churches of Asia Minor. However, modern scholars note significant differences in style and theology between Revelation and the other Johannine writings, suggesting that John of Patmos may have been a different individual altogether.

Whether apostle, prophet, or church leader, John's exile to Patmos reflects the turbulent times in which Revelation was written. Likely composed during the reign of the Roman Emperor Domitian (AD 81–96), a period marked by the persecution of Christians and the rise of the emperor cult, Revelation speaks to the challenges faced by believers in a hostile world. John's exile was not merely an act of punishment but a testament to his unwavering commitment to his faith—a faith that found its voice in the apocalyptic visions recorded in this extraordinary book.

The precise circumstances of John's life after his exile remain unclear. Some traditions hold that he returned to Ephesus and lived to an old age, while others suggest that he remained on Patmos. Regardless of his fate, his words endure, offering timeless wisdom and hope to generations of readers.

A MESSAGE FOR EVERY GENERATION

Revelation has long been a source of fascination and, at times, controversy. Written in a period of immense persecution for the early Christian church, it speaks to the struggle of faith in the face of adversity. The Roman Empire's oppression of believers, coupled with societal corruption and moral decay, provides the historical backdrop for John's vision. Yet, the message of Revelation transcends its immediate context. Its themes of endurance, divine justice, and ultimate renewal resonate across ages, offering guidance and hope for every generation.

For modern readers, Revelation speaks directly to the challenges of our time. In a world marked by division, environmental crisis, and uncertainty, its imagery of cosmic conflict mirrors the struggles we face. But it also offers the assurance that even amid chaos, a greater plan is at work—a plan rooted in love, justice, and the unshakable promise of renewal.

Revelation is not just a text for the past or the future; it is profoundly relevant to the present. It invites us to reflect on our lives, our choices, and our role in the unfolding story of creation. It challenges us to confront the forces of fear and division and to align ourselves with the enduring values of grace and compassion.

THE POWER OF SYMBOLISM

At first glance, Revelation's imagery can seem overwhelming. The beasts, seals, trumpets, and bowls may appear foreign or even frightening. Yet, these symbols are not meant to obscure Revelation's message; they are designed to illuminate it. They serve as metaphors for the spiritual realities of life, illustrating the cosmic struggle between good and evil, the consequences of human choices, and the hope of divine intervention.

Take, for example, the Lamb, central to Revelation's narrative. Depicted as slain yet triumphant, the Lamb represents Jesus Christ, embodying both sacrifice and victory. It reminds us that true power lies not in domination but in humility and love. Similarly, the Dragon symbolizes chaos and opposition to divine order, a reflection of the fears and challenges we face in our personal and collective lives. The New Jerusalem, a city of light and healing, offers a vision of the world as it could be—renewed, just, and united under the guidance of divine love.

These symbols are not confined to the pages of Revelation; they resonate with our lived experiences. They challenge us to see the spiritual dimensions of our struggles and to trust in the transformative power of grace.

AN INVITATION TO REFLECT

As you read Revelation, I invite you to set aside preconceived notions of fear or confusion. Approach it not as a puzzle to solve but as a story to experience—a story that speaks to the heart as much as to the mind. Allow its symbols to resonate with your own journey, its themes to challenge your perspectives, and its promises to inspire your faith.

Revelation is not just a text of endings but of beginnings. It is a reminder that even in the face of chaos, light prevails. It is a call to live with courage, to act with compassion, and to trust in the enduring power of divine love. Above all, it is an invitation to participate in the ongoing story of renewal—a story in which we all have a part to play.

Let us journey together into the heart of Revelation, not with fear but with hope. Let us embrace its message of grace and transformation, trusting that its truths can guide us through the challenges of today and into the promise of tomorrow.

PROLOGUE

UNVEILING THE MYSTERY OF REVELATION

The Book of Revelation has long fascinated and perplexed readers. Its vivid imagery, dramatic visions, and apocalyptic tone have made it one of the most discussed—and misunderstood—books of the Bible. For many, Revelation is shrouded in fear, seen as a forewarning of catastrophe and divine judgment. But this perception misses the heart of its message. Revelation is not a book of fear; it is a book of hope, transformation, and renewal.

At its core, Revelation is a love story—a divine invitation to trust in the enduring power of grace, even in the face of chaos. It is a call to reflect on who we are, how we live, and how we can participate in the renewal of our world. To understand Revelation is to embrace its profound message: that light always overcomes darkness, and that all things can be made new.

REVELATION IN HISTORICAL CONTEXT

To fully appreciate the Book of Revelation, it is essential to understand the world in which it was written. In the late first century, the Roman Empire was a dominant and oppressive force, persecuting early Christians who refused to worship the emperor as a god. The author of Revelation, traditionally identified as John of Patmos, wrote during this time of suffering and uncertainty. His visions were a response to the struggles of his community, offering hope to those facing persecution and urging them to remain faithful.

The imagery in Revelation—its beasts, seals, and trumpets—reflects the realities of Roman oppression and the resilience of the Christian faith. The book's symbolism, while rooted in its historical context, carries universal truths that resonate far beyond its time. Revelation speaks to all who face injustice, all who seek renewal, and all who long for the triumph of love over fear.

THE POWER OF SYMBOLISM

One of the most striking features of Revelation is its use of symbolism. From the Lamb to the Dragon, from the New Jerusalem to the River of Life, its images are rich with meaning. These symbols are not meant to be taken literally but are spiritual metaphors, designed to inspire reflection and reveal deeper truths.

For example:

- The **Lamb** symbolizes sacrifice, humility, and divine love.
- The **Dragon** represents chaos, fear, and the forces that oppose renewal.
- The **New Jerusalem** is a vision of unity, peace, and the ultimate promise of grace.

By approaching these symbols with an open heart, we can uncover their relevance to our own lives. Revelation's imagery challenges us to see beyond the surface, inviting us to engage with its messages in personal and transformative ways.

Common Misconceptions About Revelation

Revelation is often misunderstood, leading to fear-based interpretations that distort its message. Here are some common misconceptions—and the truths that counter them:

1. **Misconception**: Revelation is a prediction of the end of the world. **Truth**: Revelation is not about destruction but renewal. Its visions of judgment are not final; they are pathways to transformation. The dramatic events described in Revelation symbolize the breaking down of old systems and the purification necessary for a new beginning. Rather than foretelling doom, Revelation offers hope, assuring us that every ending carries the promise of renewal.
2. **Misconception**: Revelation is a book of fear and condemnation. **Truth**: At its heart, Revelation is a book of grace and love. While its imagery can be unsettling, its ultimate message is one of divine

care and restoration. It reminds us that even in the face of trials, God's presence is unwavering, and the story of humanity ends not in despair but in the New Jerusalem—a vision of eternal peace and unity.

3. **Misconception**: Revelation's symbols should be interpreted literally.
   Truth: The symbols in Revelation are deeply metaphorical, designed to convey spiritual truths. The beasts, the seals, the trumpets, and the bowls are not literal events but representations of human and cosmic struggles. They invite us to reflect on the forces at work in our world and to align ourselves with the values of love, justice, and renewal.
4. **Misconception**: Revelation is only relevant to its historical context.
   Truth: While Revelation was written for a specific time and place, its themes are timeless. The struggles between good and evil, truth and deception, fear and faith, are as relevant today as they were in John's time. Revelation speaks to all generations, offering guidance and hope in the face of uncertainty.
5. **Misconception**: Revelation is meant to instill fear of divine punishment.
   Truth: The judgments in Revelation are not about punishment for its own sake but about awakening humanity to its potential for transformation. They reveal the consequences of living out of alignment with divine love and invite us to embrace renewal. The text is a call to action, not a condemnation.

BY ADDRESSING THESE MISCONCEPTIONS

By addressing these misconceptions, we can approach Revelation with fresh eyes, free from fear, and open to its profound wisdom. Revelation is not a cryptic code to be deciphered, nor a tale meant to frighten its readers into submission. Instead, it is a spiritual masterpiece, filled with layers of meaning that invite us into a deeper understanding of divine love and purpose.

Revelation asks us to see beyond its dramatic imagery to the truths it reveals about the human condition and the promise of renewal. It challenges us to reflect on our own lives, our choices, and the ways we engage with the world. Far from being a story of destruction, Revelation is a divine roadmap—a guide to navigating life's challenges with courage, faith, and grace.

As we journey through its pages, we are called to co-create a world of love, justice, and unity. Revelation reminds us that even in the face of chaos and uncertainty, the promise of renewal is always within reach. Its message is not one of despair, but of hope—a hope rooted in the eternal truth that all things can be made new.

A JOURNEY OF TRANSFORMATION

With this understanding, we can begin our journey through Revelation, not as a text of fear, but as a story of divine love and grace. Each chapter brings us closer to its ultimate promise—the vision of the New Jerusalem and the triumph of light over darkness. Let us enter this journey with open hearts and minds, ready to embrace the wisdom and renewal that Revelation offers.

CHAPTER ONE

A REVELATION OF RENEWAL

The Book of Revelation has long captivated readers with its vivid imagery and powerful symbolism. Yet, for many, it has also been a source of confusion and fear, its message overshadowed by apocalyptic warnings and scenes of judgment. But what if Revelation is not a story of destruction, but of transformation? What if, instead of focusing on endings, we could see it as a divine invitation to embrace new beginnings?

Revelation is not just the final book of the Bible; it is a timeless reminder that grace is at work in every moment of chaos. It teaches us that even when the world feels overwhelming when the weight of conflict, uncertainty, and loss seems unbearable, there is a deeper truth at play. Revelation is a story of renewal, a call to trust in the eternal light that shines even in our darkest hours.

THE BLESSING OF REVELATION

From its very first verses, Revelation offers a blessing to those who engage with its message: *"Blessed is the one who reads aloud the words of this prophecy, and blessed are those who hear it and take to heart what is written in it."*(Revelation 1:3). This blessing sets the tone for the entire book, reminding us that its purpose is not to frighten, but to uplift. It assures us that by reading, hearing, and reflecting on its words, we can uncover the grace and wisdom it holds.

But why does Revelation begin with a blessing? Because its message is both challenging and transformative. It asks us to confront uncomfortable truths about ourselves and the world around us. It invites us to examine the forces of fear, division, and injustice that shape our lives. And it challenges us to see beyond these forces, to imagine a world renewed by love and grace.

A JOURNEY OF TRANSFORMATION

At its heart, Revelation is a journey—a journey through the struggles and trials of the human experience toward the promise of divine renewal. Its symbols and stories speak to universal truths that resonate as deeply today as they did when they were written. Consider some of its most iconic images:

- **The Seven Seals** reveal the cycles of struggle and perseverance that define life, reminding us that challenges are a part of the path to growth.
- **The Four Horsemen** symbolize the forces of conquest, war, scarcity, and death, inviting us to reflect on the ways these forces manifest in our world and our lives.
- **The New Jerusalem** stands as a vision of hope, a reminder that no matter how great the trials we face, grace will prevail, and renewal is always possible.

Each of these symbols is a guidepost on Revelation's journey, pointing us toward a deeper understanding of life, faith, and the power of divine love.

REVELATION IN MODERN TIMES

Though Revelation was written nearly two thousand years ago, its themes feel strikingly relevant today. We live in a world that often seems defined by conflict and uncertainty. From global crises like climate change and political unrest to personal struggles of loss and doubt, it can be easy to feel as though we are living through our own apocalyptic moments.

Yet, Revelation reminds us that chaos is not the end. It is part of the process of transformation. Just as the storms of life can strip away what no longer serves us, they also prepare the ground for new growth. Revelation calls us to see beyond the turmoil, to recognize the potential for renewal that lies within every challenge.

Consider the Four Horsemen. While they represent the forces of destruction, they also invite us to examine the ways we can confront and overcome these forces in our own lives. How do we respond to the forces of division, greed, or fear that threaten to consume us? Are we contributing to the chaos, or are we working to create a world rooted in compassion and justice?

THE PROMISE OF RENEWAL

At the heart of Revelation is the promise that all things can be made new. This is not just a distant hope for the future; it is a truth for the present moment. Renewal is not something that happens to us—it is something we are called to participate in. Revelation invites us to become co-creators of the New Jerusalem, to work toward a world where love, justice, and unity prevail.

This call to renewal is both deeply personal and profoundly communal. On a personal level, it asks us to reflect on the ways we can align our lives with grace, letting go of fear and embracing love. On a communal level, it challenges us to build communities that reflect the values of the New Jerusalem, creating spaces of healing, inclusivity, and hope.

A NEW BEGINNING

As we embark on this journey through Revelation, let us approach it with open hearts and minds. Let us see its symbols not as distant or abstract, but as reflections of the struggles and triumphs we experience in our own lives. And let us trust in its ultimate promise: that no matter how great the challenges we face, grace will prevail, and renewal is always possible.

This is the heart of Revelation's message, and the heart of this book: that even in the face of darkness, light endures. Even in the midst of chaos, there is hope. And even in the shadow of death, there is the promise of new life.

Revelation is not just a story about the end of the world; it is a story about the transformation of the human spirit. It is an invitation to trust, to hope, and to begin again. As we take our first steps on this journey, let us carry its blessing with us: the blessing of renewal, of love, and of the eternal promise that *all things can be made new*.

CHAPTER TWO

THE SEVEN CHURCHES—A MESSAGE FOR EVERY SOUL

The Book of Revelation begins not with images of judgment or visions of the New Jerusalem, but with messages to seven churches, each representing a distinct community of faith. These letters, addressed to the churches in Ephesus, Smyrna, Pergamum, Thyatira, Sardis, Philadelphia, and Laodicea, serve as spiritual diagnostics, revealing strengths, weaknesses, and areas in need of transformation. While these letters were written for specific communities, their messages resonate across time, speaking to the challenges, hopes, and struggles of every believer.

Through these letters, Revelation reminds us that the path to renewal begins with reflection. Before we can embrace the promise of the New Jerusalem, we must first examine ourselves—our values, our choices, and the ways we engage with the world around us. The letters to the seven churches call us to look inward, confront our flaws with honesty, and recommit to living in alignment with divine truth.

EPHESUS: REKINDLING OUR FIRST LOVE

The letter to the church in Ephesus begins with praise: *"I know your deeds, your hard work, and your perseverance."*(Revelation 2:2). Yet, despite their dedication, the Ephesians are admonished for having abandoned their first love. This message serves as a reminder that even the most diligent efforts can become hollow if they are not rooted in love.

For modern readers, Ephesus's message invites us to reflect on our motivations. Are we living out of obligation, or are we inspired by love? Have we become so focused on doing what is right that we have forgotten why we began in the first place? Rekindling our first love—whether it be for our faith, our relationships, or our purpose—

require us to reconnect with what truly matters and let love guide our actions.

SMYRNA: FAITHFULNESS IN THE FACE OF SUFFERING

The church in Smyrna is praised for its endurance amidst suffering: *"I know your afflictions and your poverty—yet you are rich."* (Revelation 2:9). Unlike some of the other churches, Smyrna receives no rebuke, only encouragement to remain faithful even in the face of trials.

Smyrna's story reminds us that our worth is not determined by material wealth or worldly success but by the strength of our character and the depth of our faith. It calls us to trust in the enduring power of grace, even when life feels overwhelming. For those facing hardship, the message to Smyrna is one of hope: that suffering, while painful, can lead to profound transformation and renewal.

PERGAMUM: GUARDING AGAINST COMPROMISE

The church in Pergamum is commended for remaining true to their faith despite living in a city described as the throne of Satan. Yet, they are warned against tolerating teachings that lead to compromise: *"Nevertheless, I have a few things against you."* (Revelation 2:14).

Pergamum's struggle is one of discernment—a challenge that remains deeply relevant today. In a world filled with competing voices and values, it can be easy to lose sight of what is true. The message to Pergamum calls us to remain vigilant, guard against influences that pull us away from our highest principles, and stay rooted in integrity.

THYATIRA: THE CALL TO ACCOUNTABILITY

Thyatira is praised for its love, faith, service, and perseverance, but rebuked for tolerating corruption and moral compromise: *"You tolerate that woman Jezebel, who calls herself a prophet."* (Revelation 2:20). This message speaks to the importance of accountability—both within ourselves and within our communities.

For modern readers, Thyatira's story reminds us that love and perseverance are not enough if we fail to confront harm. Whether it's addressing injustice, speaking out against dishonesty, or challenging unhealthy behaviors, accountability is essential to growth and renewal.

SARDIS: AWAKEN FROM COMPLACENCY

The letter to Sardis begins with a stark warning: *"You have a reputation of being alive, but you are dead."* (Revelation 3:1). This rebuke highlights the danger of complacency—of going through the motions without true engagement or purpose.

For those who feel stuck or disconnected, the message to Sardis is a wake-up call. It invites us to reflect on the ways we may have become complacent and to take steps to reignite our passion and purpose. Renewal begins with awakening, and Sardis reminds us that it is never too late to begin again.

PHILADELPHIA: STRENGTH IN FAITHFULNESS

The church in Philadelphia is described as having little strength, yet it is praised for remaining faithful: *"I have placed before you an open door that no one can shut."* (Revelation 3:8). This message celebrates the power of perseverance and the promise that faithfulness, even in the face of weakness, is never in vain.

Philadelphia's story encourages us to trust in the opportunities grace provides, even when we feel unequipped to take them. It reminds us that divine strength is made perfect in our weakness and that faithfulness, no matter how small, has the power to transform.

LAODICEA: THE DANGER OF LUKEWARM FAITH

The final letter, addressed to the church in Laodicea, offers a scathing critique: *"You are neither cold nor hot. I wish you were either one or the other!"* (Revelation 3:15). This image of lukewarm faith speaks to the dangers of apathy and indifference—of living without conviction or passion.

For modern readers, Laodicea's message is a call to action. It challenges us to examine the areas of our lives where we have settled for mediocrity and to rekindle our commitment to what truly matters. It reminds us that transformation requires engagement and that apathy is the greatest barrier to renewal.

A COLLECTIVE CALL TO RENEWAL

The messages to the seven churches are not just historical letters; they are timeless invitations to reflect, grow, and renew. Each church represents a different aspect of the human experience—our strengths, our struggles, and our potential for transformation.

As we read these letters, let us see them not as judgments, but as opportunities for growth. Let us take their lessons to heart, reflecting on the ways we can rekindle our love, persevere through trials, remain vigilant against compromise, and awaken from complacency. And let us trust in the promise that grace is always at work, guiding us toward renewal and the eternal light of the New Jerusalem.

CHAPTER THREE

THE SEVEN SEALS—LESSONS FROM THE SCROLL OF DESTINY

As the narrative of Revelation unfolds, the focus shifts to a pivotal moment in heaven: a scroll sealed with seven seals. This scroll, held in the right hand of the One seated on the throne, represents the unfolding of God's plan for humanity—a plan that is both mysterious and transformative. The seven seals act as a gateway to deeper truths, revealing the trials, challenges, and ultimate renewal that lie at the heart of Revelation's message.

When the question arises, *"Who is worthy to open the scroll and break its seals?"* (Revelation 5:2), the answer comes not in the form of power or conquest but in the form of a Lamb, standing as though slain. This moment reminds us that true power lies not in domination but in sacrifice, humility, and love. As the Lamb begins to open the seals, each one unveils a new layer of insight into the human experience, offering lessons that are as relevant today as they were in John's time.

THE FIRST SEAL: THE WHITE HORSE OF CONQUEST

"I looked, and there before me was a white horse! Its rider held a bow, and he was given a crown, and he rode out as a conqueror bent on conquest." (Revelation 6:2)

The rider of the white horse is often interpreted as a symbol of conquest—both literal and metaphorical. In a world driven by ambition, the white horse serves as a reminder of the allure and consequences of pursuing power for its own sake. While conquest can bring temporary victories, it often leaves a trail of division, conflict, and unfulfilled promises.

In our modern lives, the white horse challenges us to reflect on the ways we seek control or dominance, whether in personal relationships, careers, or societal systems. It asks us to consider: Are our pursuits driven by love and purpose, or by a desire for power and recognition? True renewal begins when we shift our focus from conquest to collaboration, from dominance to service.

THE SECOND SEAL: THE RED HORSE OF WAR

"Then another horse came out, a fiery red one. Its rider was given the power to take peace from the earth and to make people kill each other. To him was given a large sword." (Revelation 6:4)

The red horse represents the destructive force of conflict, both external and internal. It reminds us of the toll that division and hostility take on individuals, communities, and nations. While conflict is an inevitable part of the human experience, the red horse warns against allowing it to consume us.

Today, the red horse can be seen in global conflicts, political polarization, and personal disagreements. Its presence calls us to become peacemakers, to seek resolution and understanding even in the midst of tension. It reminds us that true strength lies not in perpetuating conflict but in fostering reconciliation and unity.

THE THIRD SEAL: THE BLACK HORSE OF SCARCITY

"I looked, and there before me was a black horse! Its rider was holding a pair of scales in his hand." (Revelation 6:5)

The black horse symbolizes scarcity and economic imbalance, a theme that resonates deeply in a world where inequality persists. The image of the scales reminds us of the delicate balance required to ensure fairness and justice, particularly when resources are limited.

In our modern context, the black horse challenges us to reflect on issues such as poverty, wealth disparity, and environmental sustainability. It invites us to consider how we use our resources and whether we are contributing to a more equitable world. By addressing scarcity with compassion and generosity, we can work toward a vision of abundance that aligns with the values of the New Jerusalem.

THE FOURTH SEAL: THE PALE HORSE OF DEATH

"I looked, and there before me was a pale horse! Its rider was named Death, and Hades was following close behind him."(Revelation 6:8)

The pale horse represents the inevitability of death—a reality that unites all of humanity. While death is often seen as an end, Revelation reframes it as a transition, a sacred passage that leads to renewal and transformation.

For modern readers, the pale horse reminds us to live with intention, embracing each moment as an opportunity to create meaning and connection. It encourages us to confront our fears of mortality and trust in the promise of eternal renewal.

THE FIFTH SEAL: THE CRY OF THE MARTYRS

"I saw under the altar the souls of those who had been slain because of the word of God and the testimony they had maintained." (Revelation 6:9)

The opening of the fifth seal shifts the focus from earthly trials to the voices of those who have suffered for their faith. The martyrs' cry—"How long, Sovereign Lord, holy and true, until you judge the inhabitants of the earth and avenge our blood?"—speaks to the universal longing for justice.

In today's world, the cry of the martyrs resonates with the voices of those who have been marginalized, oppressed, or silenced. Their testimony reminds us of the importance of standing up for truth and justice, even in the face of adversity. It calls us to honor their legacy by working toward a more just and compassionate world.

THE SIXTH SEAL: COSMIC DISTURBANCES

"There was a great earthquake. The sun turned black like sackcloth made of goat hair, the whole moon turned blood red, and the stars in the sky fell to earth." (Revelation 6:12–13)

The sixth seal unveils a scene of cosmic upheaval, symbolizing the breaking apart of old systems and the preparation for something new. These disturbances are not merely destructive; they are transformative, paving the way for renewal.

For modern readers, the sixth seal challenges us to see disruption as an opportunity for growth. Whether it's a personal crisis or a societal shift, moments of upheaval often lead to deeper understanding and change. The sixth seal invites us to trust in the process of transformation, even when it feels overwhelming.

THE SEVENTH SEAL: SILENCE IN HEAVEN

"When he opened the seventh seal, there was silence in heaven for about half an hour." (Revelation 8:1)

Unlike the others, the seventh seal does not reveal an immediate event but ushers in a profound silence. This moment of stillness invites reflection, reminding us that silence is often where the deepest truths are found.

In a world filled with noise and distractions, the seventh seal encourages us to create space for stillness in our own lives. It is in these quiet moments that we can connect with the divine, find clarity, and prepare for the renewal that lies ahead.

LESSONS FROM THE SEVEN SEALS

The seven seals are more than a sequence of events; they are a journey through the trials and triumphs of the human experience. They remind us that while life is marked by challenges—conflict, scarcity, loss—these trials are not the end of the story. They are part of the process of transformation, leading us toward the light of the New Jerusalem.

As we reflect on the lessons of the seals, let us embrace their call to live with intention, courage, and compassion. Let us trust that even in the midst of struggle, grace is at work, guiding us toward renewal and the eternal promise that all things can be made new.

CHAPTER FOUR

THE SEVEN TRUMPETS—A CALL TO TRANSFORMATION

As the seventh seal is opened, a new series of events unfolds, the sounding of the seven trumpets. These trumpets act as divine wake-up calls, each announcing a moment of reckoning and reflection. Unlike the seals, which focus on the trials and transitions of human existence, the trumpets draw attention to humanity's relationship with creation, justice, and the divine. They are not final judgments but opportunities for transformation, urging humanity to respond with humility, reverence, and action.

Each trumpet represents a moment of disruption, a call to examine the state of our world and our hearts. They remind us that transformation often begins with discomfort, as old systems break apart to make way for renewal. The trumpets invite us to listen deeply, reflect on the lessons they bring, and respond with courage and grace.

THE FIRST TRUMPET: HAIL, FIRE, AND BLOOD

"The first angel sounded his trumpet, and there came hail and fire mixed with blood, and it was hurled down on the earth. A third of the earth was burned up." (Revelation 8:7)

The first trumpet signals a disruption in the natural world, with hail and fire descending upon the earth and causing widespread destruction. This imagery serves as a stark reminder of humanity's interconnectedness with creation. The burning of the earth points to the consequences of exploitation and neglect, challenging us to reflect on our role as stewards of the environment.

In our modern context, the first trumpet resonates deeply as we face environmental crises such as deforestation, climate change, and pollution. It calls us to take responsibility for the care of the planet, recognizing that our actions have far-reaching consequences. The first trumpet is not just a warning but an invitation to align our lives with principles of sustainability, respect, and care for the earth.

THE SECOND TRUMPET: A BLAZING MOUNTAIN

"The second angel sounded his trumpet, and something like a huge mountain, all ablaze, was thrown into the sea."(Revelation 8:8)

The image of a blazing mountain plunging into the sea evokes a sense of chaos and upheaval. A third of the sea turns to blood, devastating marine life and disrupting the balance of creation. This trumpet symbolizes the collapse of systems that once seemed immovable, reminding us that even the most powerful structures are vulnerable to change.

For modern readers, the second trumpet challenges us to examine the systems and structures we rely on, from economic institutions to political regimes. It asks us to consider: Are these systems serving the greater good, or are they contributing to inequality and harm? The second trumpet reminds us that transformation often requires dismantling what no longer serves, creating space for new and just systems to emerge.

THE THIRD TRUMPET: THE STAR WORMWOOD

"The third angel sounded his trumpet, and a great star, blazing like a torch, fell from the sky on a third of the rivers and on the springs of water." (Revelation 8:10)

The star Wormwood falls from the sky, poisoning the waters and making them bitter. This trumpet speaks to the consequences of corruption and neglect, particularly in the context of resources that sustain life. The bitter waters symbolize the contamination of what should be pure and life-giving.

In today's world, the third trumpet calls attention to issues such as water scarcity, pollution, and the exploitation of natural resources. It invites us to reflect on how we value and protect the essential elements of life, both physical and spiritual. The bitterness of

Wormwood is a reminder that renewal begins with healing—of our environment, our relationships, and our hearts.

THE FOURTH TRUMPET: DARKNESS OVER THE EARTH

"The fourth angel sounded his trumpet, and a third of the sun was struck, a third of the moon, and a third of the stars so that a third of them turned dark." (Revelation 8:12)

The fourth trumpet brings darkness, with the light of the sun, moon, and stars diminished by a third. This disruption of celestial order reflects a loss of guidance, clarity, and hope, plunging the world into uncertainty.

For modern readers, this trumpet resonates with moments of personal or collective darkness—times when direction and purpose seem obscured. It challenges us to seek the light even in the midst of shadow, trusting that divine wisdom and grace are always present, even when they feel hidden. The fourth trumpet reminds us that darkness is not permanent and that clarity will return in time.

THE FIFTH TRUMPET: THE ABYSS OPENS

"The fifth angel sounded his trumpet, and I saw a star that had fallen from the sky to the earth. The star was given the key to the shaft of the Abyss." (Revelation 9:1)

The fifth trumpet unleashes a plague of locusts from the Abyss, tormenting humanity but not killing them. This vivid imagery symbolizes the internal and external forces that torment and oppress, creating a state of suffering without resolution.

In our modern lives, the fifth trumpet invites us to confront the sources of torment in our own hearts and communities. Whether it's anxiety, division, or systemic injustice, the locusts of the Abyss remind us of the importance of addressing these challenges with courage and compassion. They also underscore the need for collective healing, as individual struggles often reflect broader societal wounds.

THE SIXTH TRUMPET: A CALL TO REPENTANCE

"The sixth angel sounded his trumpet, and four angels who had been kept ready for this very hour, day, month, and year were released to kill a third of mankind." (Revelation 9:15)

The sixth trumpet introduces a moment of reckoning, as forces are unleashed that lead to widespread devastation. Yet, despite the destruction, humanity does not repent of its actions or turn toward renewal. This trumpet highlights the consequences of stubbornness, apathy, and resistance to change.

For modern readers, the sixth trumpet is a call to self-awareness and transformation. It challenges us to recognize the patterns and behaviors that contribute to harm and to take meaningful steps toward change. The sixth trumpet reminds us that transformation begins with humility and the willingness to grow.

THE SEVENTH TRUMPET: THE KINGDOM OF GOD

"The seventh angel sounded his trumpet, and there were loud voices in heaven, which said: 'The kingdom of the world has become the kingdom of our Lord and of his Messiah, and he will reign forever and ever.'" (Revelation 11:15)

The seventh trumpet marks a turning point, announcing the triumph of God's kingdom and the ultimate renewal of creation. It is a moment of celebration, signaling the fulfillment of divine promises and the restoration of harmony.

For modern readers, the seventh trumpet offers a vision of hope and purpose. It reminds us that the struggles and challenges we face are not the end of the story. The seventh trumpet invites us to participate in the work of renewal, co-creating a world where love, justice, and unity prevail.

LESSONS FROM THE TRUMPETS

The seven trumpets are not just warnings; they are calls to action. They challenge us to reflect on our relationship with creation, our communities, and ourselves. They remind us that transformation often begins with disruption and that renewal requires both reflection and action.

As we listen to the trumpets' call, let us embrace their lessons with open hearts. Let us work to heal the wounds of the earth, to create systems of justice and compassion, and to live with the courage to confront darkness with light. For in the sound of the trumpets, we hear not only the challenges of our time but also the promise of a world made new.

CHAPTER FIVE

THE WOMAN, THE DRAGON, AND THE BEASTS— THE STRUGGLE BETWEEN GOOD AND EVIL

As Revelation unfolds, the narrative takes a dramatic turn. We are introduced to the Woman and the Dragon—a vivid and symbolic tale that portrays the cosmic struggle between good and evil. This story, followed by the emergence of two Beasts, reveals the challenges and choices humanity faces in the battle between truth and deception, hope and fear, love and power. These symbols transcend their historical context, offering timeless insights into the forces that shape our world and our lives.

The Woman, the Dragon, and the Beasts remind us that while the battle between good and evil is inevitable, the ultimate victory belongs to love, grace, and renewal. This chapter calls us to reflect on how these forces manifest in our own experiences and invites us to choose the path of courage, compassion, and faith.

THE WOMAN CLOTHED WITH THE SUN

"A great sign appeared in heaven: a woman clothed with the sun, with the moon under her feet and a crown of twelve stars on her head. She was pregnant and cried out in pain as she was about to give birth." (Revelation 12:1–2)

The Woman, clothed in celestial splendor, represents purity, resilience, and the promise of new beginnings. Often interpreted as a symbol of the Church, Israel, or even the divine feminine, she embodies the nurturing power of creation and the hope that arises in the midst of struggle.

Her labor reflects the universal experience of bringing forth something new, whether it's a vision, a mission, or a personal transformation. The pain of childbirth reminds us that growth and renewal often come with challenges, yet her ultimate victory assures us that these struggles are not in vain.

THE DRAGON: THE FORCE OF OPPOSITION

"Then another sign appeared in heaven: an enormous red dragon with seven heads and ten horns and seven crowns on its heads. Its tail swept a third of the stars out of the sky and flung them to the earth." (Revelation 12:3–4)

The Dragon, a powerful and menacing figure, symbolizes the forces of chaos, fear, and oppression that seek to thwart the Woman's purpose. Its attempt to devour her child reflects the relentless efforts of evil to undermine hope and destroy what is sacred.

In our modern lives, the Dragon can represent systemic injustices, personal fears, or destructive influences that threaten to overwhelm us. Its presence challenges us to confront these forces with courage and to trust in the power of grace to overcome even the most formidable opposition.

THE CHILD AND DIVINE PROTECTION

"She gave birth to a son, a male child, who 'will rule all the nations with an iron scepter.' And her child was snatched up to God and to his throne." (Revelation 12:5)

The birth of the child signifies the emergence of hope, renewal, and divine purpose. Despite the Dragon's attempts to destroy him, the child is protected by God, symbolizing the ultimate triumph of good over evil.

For modern readers, the child represents the potential within each of us to bring about change, healing, and transformation. The story assures us that no matter how great the opposition, divine protection and grace are always present, guiding us toward our purpose.

THE WOMAN'S FLIGHT TO THE WILDERNESS

"The woman fled into the wilderness to a place prepared for her by God, where she might be taken care of for 1,260 days." (Revelation 12:6)

The Woman's flight to the wilderness highlights the interplay between vulnerability and divine care. The wilderness, often seen as a place of trial, becomes a sanctuary where she is nourished and strengthened.

In our own lives, the wilderness can represent times of uncertainty or solitude, where we are called to trust in divine provision. These moments, though challenging, often become the foundation for growth and renewal, preparing us to face life's battles with greater resilience.

THE BEASTS: FORCES OF DECEPTION AND OPPRESSION

Following the story of the Woman and the Dragon, Revelation introduces two Beasts—one from the sea and one from the earth. These Beasts symbolize the oppressive systems and deceptive influences that challenge humanity's faithfulness and integrity.

The Beast from the Sea

"The Beast I saw resembled a leopard, but had feet like those of a bear and a mouth like that of a lion." (Revelation 13:2)

The Beast from the Sea wields authority and power, demanding allegiance and instilling fear. It represents corrupt systems that exploit and oppress, drawing attention to the dangers of unchecked power.

For modern readers, this Beast serves as a warning against the allure of authoritarianism, greed, and exploitation. It calls us to remain vigilant and resist the temptation to compromise our values in the face of worldly power.

The Beast from the Earth

"It performed great signs, even causing fire to come down from heaven to the earth in full view of the people."(Revelation 13:13)

The Beast from the Earth, often seen as a false prophet, promotes deception and false worship. Its ability to perform signs and wonders highlights the danger of being swayed by appearances rather than truth.

In today's world, this Beast reminds us of the importance of discernment. Whether it's misinformation, propaganda, or manipulative influences, the Beast from the Earth challenges us to seek truth and remain grounded in integrity.

The Mark of the Beast

"It also forced all people, great and small, rich and poor, free and slave, to receive a mark on their right hands or on their foreheads." (Revelation 13:16)

The Mark of the Beast symbolizes allegiance to systems of power that oppose divine truth. It serves as a stark reminder of our choices and the values we align ourselves with.

For modern readers, the Mark challenges us to examine our own actions and priorities. Are we aligning ourselves with systems that exploit, divide, or harm? Or are we choosing to live in alignment with love, justice, and grace?

LESSONS FOR MODERN LIFE

The Woman, the Dragon, and the Beasts offer powerful insights into the challenges and choices we face:

- **Courage in the Face of Opposition**: Like the Woman, we are called to persevere in the face of fear and adversity, trusting in divine protection.
- **Discernment in the Midst of Deception**: The Beasts remind us to remain vigilant, seeking truth and integrity in a world filled with falsehoods.
- **Hope in the Promise of Renewal**: The birth of the child assures us that even in the midst of chaos, new beginnings are always possible.

A CALL TO ACTION

As we reflect on these symbols, let us embrace their lessons with open hearts. Let us stand firm in the face of opposition, nurture the potential for renewal within ourselves, and work to create a world rooted in truth and compassion. The story of the Woman, the Dragon, and the Beasts is not just a cosmic drama—it is a reflection of our own journey, calling us to live with courage, hope, and unwavering faith.

CHAPTER SIX

THE SEVEN BOWLS—THE FINAL RECKONING AND THE PATH TO RENEWAL

As the story of Revelation unfolds, the narrative crescendos with the pouring out of the seven bowls of wrath. These bowls represent a final reckoning—a series of judgments that confront humanity with the consequences of its choices. They are vivid and unsettling, filled with imagery that speaks to the weight of collective actions and the urgent need for transformation.

Yet, the bowls are not merely about destruction; they are about purification. They reveal the depth of divine justice and the lengths to which grace will go to restore balance and harmony to creation. Each bowl serves as a mirror, reflecting the ways humanity has turned away from its divine purpose, and as a call to return to a life of integrity, compassion, and truth.

THE FIRST BOWL: SORES ON THOSE WHO WORSHIP THE BEAST

"The first angel went and poured out his bowl on the land, and ugly, festering sores broke out on the people who had the mark of the beast and worshiped its image." (Revelation 16:2)

The first bowl confronts those who have aligned themselves with corrupt systems, symbolized by the mark of the beast. The festering sores represent the internal and external consequences of living out of alignment with divine truth. This imagery suggests that the choices we make affect not only the world around us but also affect our own well-being.

In a modern context, the First Bowl challenges us to reflect on the impact of our allegiances. Are we contributing to systems of exploitation, greed, or injustice? Are we compromising our values in ways that harm ourselves and others? The First Bowl invites us to realign our lives with integrity and heal the wounds caused by misplaced priorities.

THE SECOND BOWL: THE SEA TURNS TO BLOOD

"The second angel poured out his bowl on the sea, and it turned into blood like that of a dead person, and every living thing in the sea died." (Revelation 16:3)

The second bowl devastates the sea, symbolizing the destruction of creation's vitality. The sea, often seen as a source of life and sustenance, becomes a place of death, reflecting humanity's disregard for the natural world.

Today, this imagery resonates with the environmental crises we face, from pollution to the degradation of marine ecosystems. The second bowl is a stark reminder of the interconnectedness of life and the consequences of neglecting our role as stewards of the earth. It calls us to protect and restore the natural world, recognizing that the health of creation is deeply tied to our own well-being.

THE THIRD BOWL: RIVERS AND SPRINGS BECOME BLOOD

"The third angel poured out his bowl on the rivers and springs of water, and they became blood." (Revelation 16:4)

The third bowl extends the destruction to freshwater sources, emphasizing the fragility of the resources that sustain life. Blood imagery serves as a symbol of judgment, reflecting the consequences of exploitation and harm.

For modern readers, the Third Bowl speaks to issues such as water scarcity, contamination, and the unequal distribution of resources. It challenges us to value and protect the essential elements of life, ensuring that they are available for all. The Third Bowl is a call to stewardship, urging us to honor the sacredness of creation and to act with compassion and responsibility.

THE FOURTH BOWL: THE SCORCHING SUN

"The fourth angel poured out his bowl on the sun, and the sun was allowed to scorch people with fire." (Revelation 16:8)

The fourth bowl intensifies the imagery of judgment, with the sun's heat becoming a force of torment. This disruption of nature's balance reflects the consequences of humanity's actions, particularly in the context of environmental degradation and climate change.

In today's world, the fourth bowl reminds us of the urgent need to address global warming and its impacts. It calls us to action, recognizing that our choices have a profound effect on the planet. The fourth bowl is a plea for transformation, inviting us to shift from exploitation to sustainability and from indifference to care.

THE FIFTH BOWL: DARKNESS OVER THE BEAST'S KINGDOM

"The fifth angel poured out his bowl on the throne of the beast, and its kingdom was plunged into darkness." (Revelation 16:10)

The fifth bowl targets the kingdom of the beast, plunging it into darkness. This imagery symbolizes the collapse of corrupt systems and the exposure of their emptiness. The darkness reflects the absence of truth, integrity, and divine presence in these structures.

For modern readers, the Fifth Bowl challenges us to confront the systems of power and oppression that dominate our world. It invites us to participate in their dismantling, creating space for justice, equity, and renewal. The Fifth Bowl reminds us that no system built on exploitation or falsehood can endure in the light of divine truth.

THE SIXTH BOWL: THE DRYING OF THE EUPHRATES

"The sixth angel poured out his bowl on the great river Euphrates, and its water was dried up to prepare the way for the kings from the East." (Revelation 16:12)

The sixth bowl sets the stage for a final confrontation, with the drying of the Euphrates symbolizing the removal of barriers to conflict. This imagery reflects the buildup of tension and the inevitability of reckoning.

In a modern context, the sixth bowl reminds us of the need to address unresolved issues and to engage with the challenges that stand in the way of renewal. It calls us to face conflict with courage and to work toward resolution, trusting that transformation is possible even in the midst of struggle.

THE SEVENTH BOWL: THE GREAT EARTHQUAKE

"The seventh angel poured out his bowl into the air, and out of the temple came a loud voice from the throne, saying, 'It is done!'" (Revelation 16:17)

The seventh bowl concludes the series with a great earthquake, signaling the collapse of old structures and the ushering in of something new. The declaration, "It is done!", echoes the finality of transformation and the fulfillment of divine purpose.

For modern readers, the seventh bowl is a reminder that every ending is a beginning. It calls us to trust in the process of renewal, even when it feels overwhelming. The seventh bowl invites us to let go of what no longer serves us and to embrace the promise of a world made new.

LESSONS FROM THE BOWLS

The seven bowls are vivid and challenging, yet they offer profound insights into the human experience. They remind us that while transformation can be painful, it is ultimately a process of purification and renewal. Each bowl calls us to reflect on our choices, take responsibility for our actions, and participate in the healing of creation.

As we listen to the messages of the bowls, let us respond with courage and compassion. Let us work to restore balance and harmony to the world, trusting that even in the midst of reckoning, grace is at work, guiding us toward the eternal promise of renewal.

CHAPTER SEVEN

THE FALL OF BABYLON—LESSONS FROM THE COLLAPSE OF CORRUPTION

As Revelation progresses, the focus shifts to the vivid and dramatic fall of Babylon, a city depicted as the ultimate symbol of greed, corruption, and spiritual decay. Babylon is described as a city of immense power and wealth, yet its foundation is built on exploitation, immorality, and injustice. Its fall serves as a cautionary tale, illustrating the consequences of living in opposition to divine values and the inevitable collapse of systems rooted in selfishness and greed.

The story of Babylon is not just a historical or prophetic narrative; it is a timeless reminder of the dangers of placing power and wealth above compassion and integrity. It invites us to examine the "Babylons" in our own lives—whether they are societal structures, personal ambitions, or collective systems—and to reflect on how we can build a more just and compassionate world.

BABYLON THE GREAT: A SYMBOL OF CORRUPTION

*"Fallen! Fallen is Babylon the Great! She has become a dwelling for demons and a haunt for every impure spirit."(*Revelation 18:2)

Babylon is portrayed as a grand and seductive city, outwardly magnificent but inwardly corrupt. It represents the human tendency to prioritize wealth, power, and pleasure over ethical and spiritual values. Its collapse is a stark warning that no system built on exploitation and deceit can endure.

For modern readers, Babylon serves as a mirror, reflecting the aspects of our world that perpetuate inequality, greed, and harm. From economic systems that exploit the vulnerable to environmental destruction driven by unchecked consumption, the spirit of Babylon is alive in the challenges we face today. The question Revelation poses is clear: What are we building, and on what foundation?

THE MERCHANTS AND THE MOURNING

"The merchants of the earth will weep and mourn over her because no one buys their cargoes anymore." (Revelation 18:11)

The fall of Babylon is met with mourning, not for its moral failings but for the loss of profit and luxury. The merchants and kings who benefited from Babylon's corruption lament its destruction, revealing their misplaced priorities and values.

This imagery highlights the dangers of placing material wealth above human dignity and spiritual truth. In a world where consumerism often takes precedence over compassion, the fall of Babylon challenges us to reexamine our priorities. Are we building lives and systems that uplift and sustain, or are we contributing to cycles of exploitation and harm?

A CALL TO SEPARATION

"Come out of her, my people, so that you will not share in her sins so that you will not receive any of her plagues."(Revelation 18:4)

God's people are called to separate themselves from Babylon, to reject its values and practices. This call is not just about physical separation but a deeper spiritual and ethical distancing from systems and behaviors that perpetuate harm.

In modern terms, this call invites us to examine our own complicity in systems of injustice. Whether it's choosing to support ethical businesses, advocating for fair policies, or examining our personal habits, coming out of Babylon means aligning our lives with values of love, justice, and compassion. It is a call to live counter-culturally, building communities that reflect the values of the New Jerusalem rather than the corruption of Babylon.

THE FALL OF BABYLON AS A REFLECTION OF JUSTICE

"In one hour, such great wealth has been brought to ruin!" (Revelation 18:17)

The sudden and dramatic collapse of Babylon underscores the inevitability of divine justice. While it may seem that systems of corruption endure, Revelation assures us that they cannot stand forever. The fall of Babylon is not just an act of judgment; it is an act of renewal, clearing the way for the establishment of a just and harmonious world.

For those who feel disillusioned by injustice's persistence, the fall of Babylon offers hope. It reminds us that while change may be slow, the arc of divine justice is unyielding. The collapse of corruption is not just a possibility—it is an inevitability.

MODERN PARALLELS TO BABYLON

The spirit of Babylon is not confined to the ancient world; it manifests in countless ways today. Consider the following:

- **Economic Exploitation**: Systems that prioritize profit over people, perpetuating cycles of poverty and inequality.
- **Environmental Degradation**: Practices that harm the planet for the sake of short-term gain, ignoring the long-term consequences for future generations.
- **Cultural Narcissism**: A focus on appearance, power, and status that neglects deeper values of community and humility.

By recognizing these manifestations of Babylon, we are better equipped to address them, both individually and collectively. Revelation's call to "come out of her" is a challenge to build systems and lives that reflect integrity, justice, and care for creation.

A VISION OF RENEWAL

The fall of Babylon is not the end of the story; it is a precursor to renewal. As the city collapses, the stage is set for the emergence of the New Jerusalem—a city built on love, unity, and divine presence. This transition reminds us that destruction is not the goal; transformation is.

In our own lives, the fall of Babylon invites us to let go of what no longer serves us and to release attachments to power, greed, and fear. It challenges us to imagine and co-create a world where compassion, justice, and grace prevail.

LESSONS FROM THE FALL OF BABYLON

1. **Examine Your Foundations**: What are you building your life on? Are your actions and choices aligned with values of integrity and compassion, or are they rooted in fear, greed, or self-interest?
2. **Challenge Injustice**: Babylon's fall is a reminder that systems of exploitation and harm cannot endure. How can you contribute to dismantling these systems and building something better?
3. **Trust in Divine Justice**: Even when injustice seems overwhelming, Revelation assures us that grace and renewal will prevail. The fall of Babylon is not an end but a beginning.
4. **Embrace Transformation**: Like the collapse of Babylon, personal and societal transformation often requires letting go of old patterns. How can you embrace change with courage and hope?

THE CALL TO ACTION

The fall of Babylon is more than a story of judgment; it is a call to action. It challenges us to reflect on the systems we participate in, the values we uphold, and the world we are helping to create. It invites us to reject Babylon's corruption and work toward the vision of the New Jerusalem—a world of love, justice, and unity.

As we continue our journey through Revelation, let us carry the lessons of Babylon's fall with us. Let us confront the Babylon's in our own lives with courage and faith, trusting in the promise of renewal and the power of divine grace to transform even the darkest corners of our world.

CHAPTER EIGHT

THE WEDDING SUPPER OF THE LAMB—A CELEBRATION OF DIVINE UNITY

As Revelation transitions from the collapse of Babylon to the promise of renewal, we are presented with one of its most joyous and hopeful images: the Wedding Supper of the Lamb. This divine celebration marks the culmination of God's plan, a union between Christ (the Lamb) and His people, symbolized as His bride. It is a moment of victory, joy, and profound connection, emphasizing the restoration of harmony between the divine and humanity.

The Wedding Supper of the Lamb is more than a vision of celebration; it is a call to relationship. It reminds us that faith is not merely a set of beliefs or practices but a living, dynamic connection with the divine. This chapter invites us to reflect on the significance of this union and how it inspires us to live with purpose, love, and gratitude.

THE INVITATION TO THE WEDDING SUPPER

"Blessed are those who are invited to the wedding supper of the Lamb!" (Revelation 19:9)

The invitation to the Wedding Supper is universal, extending to all who accept the call to live in alignment with divine love and grace. This image of a wedding, a union built on commitment and trust, serves as a powerful metaphor for the relationship between God and humanity. It reflects a bond that is both deeply personal and profoundly communal.

In modern terms, this invitation is a reminder that we are all called to participate in the divine plan. It challenges us to embrace our role as co-creators of a world rooted in justice, compassion, and unity. The Wedding Supper is not just a future promise but an invitation to live in a divine relationship here and now.

THE BRIDE: A SYMBOL OF PURITY AND FAITHFULNESS

"Let us rejoice and be glad and give him glory! For the wedding of the Lamb has come, and his bride has made herself ready. Fine linen, bright and clean, was given her to wear." (Revelation 19:7–8)

The bride, representing the Church or the collective faithful, is adorned in fine linen, symbolizing righteousness and purity. This imagery underscores the importance of preparation and faithfulness in the journey of faith. The bride does not appear by chance; she is ready because she has embraced a life of alignment with divine truth.

For modern readers, the bride's readiness is a call to action. It asks us to reflect on how we are preparing ourselves for a divine relationship. Are we living with intention, nurturing our connection with the divine, and aligning our actions with our values? The bride's preparation is not about perfection but about commitment—a willingness to grow, transform, and live authentically.

THE LAMB: A SYMBOL OF SACRIFICE AND VICTORY

Central to the Wedding Supper is the Lamb, a recurring symbol of Christ's sacrifice, humility, and love. The Lamb's presence at this celebration reminds us that divine unity is made possible through grace. It is not something we earn but something we receive as a gift.

For modern readers, the Lamb challenges us to embrace the values of humility, compassion, and service. It calls us to live in a way that reflects the sacrificial love that makes divine unity possible. The Wedding Supper is a reminder that victory is not achieved through power or domination but through love and grace.

THE JOY OF THE CELEBRATION

The Wedding Supper of the Lamb is a moment of pure joy, a celebration of love, unity, and renewal. It marks the fulfillment of divine promises and the beginning of a new chapter in the relationship between God and humanity. The imagery of a feast emphasizes abundance, connection, and shared purpose.

For modern readers, this celebration invites us to reflect on the importance of joy and gratitude in our lives. It challenges us to create moments of celebration, nurture relationships, and recognize the blessings that surround us. The Wedding Supper is a vision of divine abundance, reminding us that we are called to live with open hearts and generous spirits.

THE CONTRAST WITH BABYLON

The Wedding Supper stands in stark contrast to the fall of Babylon. Where Babylon represents corruption, greed, and isolation, the Wedding Supper symbolizes purity, love, and connection. This juxtaposition highlights the choices we face in our own lives: to align with the values of Babylon or to embrace the invitation to the Wedding Supper.

For modern readers, this contrast serves as a reminder of the importance of alignment and intention. It asks us to reflect on the values that guide our lives and to choose paths that lead to connection, renewal, and divine relationships.

A UNIVERSAL VISION

The Wedding Supper of the Lamb is not limited to any one group or tradition; it is a universal vision of unity and inclusion. Its invitation is extended to all who seek to live in alignment with divine love. This inclusivity reflects the heart of Revelation's message: that grace is for everyone, and that the promise of renewal transcends boundaries of culture, nationality, and belief.

For modern readers, this universal vision challenges us to build communities that reflect the inclusivity of the Wedding Supper. It calls us to break down barriers, to celebrate diversity, and to create spaces where everyone is welcomed and valued.

LESSONS FROM THE WEDDING SUPPER

1. **Embrace the Invitation**: The Wedding Supper reminds us that we are all invited into the divine relationship. How are you responding to this invitation in your own life? Are you living with intention and purpose, nurturing your connection with the divine?
2. **Celebrate Abundance**: The feast imagery challenges us to live with gratitude and generosity. How can you create moments of celebration and connection in your daily life? How can you share your blessings with others?
3. **Reflect on Alignment**: The contrast with Babylon invites us to reflect on our values and priorities. Are you living in alignment with love, justice, and grace, or are there areas where you need to make changes?
4. **Build Inclusive Communities**: The universal vision of the Wedding Supper challenges us to create spaces of inclusion and unity. How can you contribute to building communities that reflect the values of love and connection?

THE CALL TO JOY

The Wedding Supper of the Lamb is a celebration of divine unity, a moment of profound joy and connection. It reminds us that faith is not about fear or obligation but about relationship, love, and renewal. As we reflect on this vision, let us carry its lessons into our own lives, creating moments of joy, nurturing relationships, and living with open hearts.

Revelation assures us that humanity's story is one of hope and renewal. The Wedding Supper is not just a vision of the future; it is an invitation to live with purpose and joy in the present. Let us embrace this invitation, trusting in the promise of divine grace and the eternal truth that love always prevails.

CHAPTER NINE

THE FINAL BATTLE—THE TRIUMPH OF LIGHT OVER DARKNESS

As Revelation draws closer to its climax, we are taken to the scene of the final battle: the ultimate confrontation between good and evil, truth and deception, light and darkness. This moment, filled with vivid imagery and dramatic tension, represents the culmination of humanity's spiritual journey. It is not simply a physical war but a cosmic reckoning, a decisive moment in which the forces of love and grace triumph over fear and corruption.

The final battle is not about destruction; it is about restoration. It symbolizes the end of old, broken systems and the emergence of divine order, a world renewed by truth and justice. This chapter invites us to explore the deeper meaning of this confrontation and to reflect on its relevance to our own lives.

THE RIDER ON THE WHITE HORSE

"I saw heaven standing open and there before me was a white horse, whose rider is called Faithful and True. With justice he judges and wages war." (Revelation 19:11)

At the center of the final battle is the Rider on the White Horse, a figure of unwavering righteousness and divine authority. His name, "Faithful and True," underscores his role as the embodiment of truth, justice, and grace. Unlike earthly conquerors, his power comes not from domination but from his alignment with divine purpose.

For modern readers, the Rider represents the call to live with integrity and courage. He challenges us to confront the forces of deception and fear in our own lives and to stand firm in the pursuit of truth and justice. The white horse reminds us that victory is not achieved through aggression but through a steadfast commitment to what is right.

THE SWORD OF HIS MOUTH

"Coming out of his mouth is a sharp sword with which to strike down the nations." (Revelation 19:15)

The Rider's sword, described as coming from his mouth, symbolizes the power of truth and the Word of God. This imagery highlights the transformative power of words—both divine and human—and their ability to challenge injustice and inspire renewal.

In a world where misinformation and manipulation often dominate, the sword of truth reminds us of the importance of speaking and living authentically. It calls us to use our words to uplift, to heal, and to bring clarity in the midst of confusion. The sword is not a weapon of destruction but a tool of transformation.

THE DEFEAT OF THE BEAST AND THE FALSE PROPHET

"The beast was captured, and with it the false prophet who had performed the signs on its behalf." (Revelation 19:20)

The final battle culminates in the defeat of the Beast and the False Prophet, symbols of corruption and deception. Their downfall marks the end of systems and ideologies that oppose divine truth and perpetuate harm.

For modern readers, the fall of these figures serves as a reminder that no force of corruption can endure in the presence of grace. It invites us to reflect on the systems and influences in our own lives that need to be dismantled and to trust in the power of truth to prevail.

THE BINDING OF SATAN

"He seized the dragon, that ancient serpent, who is the devil, or Satan, and bound him for a thousand years." (Revelation 20:2)

The binding of Satan represents the temporary restraint of evil, a moment of peace and restoration. This image emphasizes the ultimate power of the divine over all forces of chaos and destruction. The thousand years, often called the Millennium, symbolize a period of renewal and divine governance.

For modern readers, this moment offers hope that even in times of struggle, evil does not have the final word. It challenges us to participate in the work of renewal, creating spaces of peace and justice where the forces of chaos are held at bay.

THE ROLE OF HUMANITY IN THE FINAL BATTLE

While the imagery of the final battle focuses on divine action, humanity is not a passive observer. The faithful are called to witness, to persevere, and to align themselves with the values of truth and justice. The battle is as much an internal struggle as it is a cosmic one, reflecting the choices each of us must make in our daily lives.

For modern readers, this battle invites reflection on how we contribute to the triumph of light over darkness. How do our actions, choices, and words reflect our commitment to truth? How are we participating in the work of restoration and renewal?

THE MEANING OF VICTORY

The victory in the final battle is not about destruction but about restoration. It marks the end of corruption, deception, and fear, clearing the way for the New Jerusalem. This victory is rooted in love, not power; in grace, not force. It is a reminder that the ultimate triumph of good over evil is not just a cosmic promise but a present reality, unfolding in our lives and in the world around us.

LESSONS FROM THE FINAL BATTLE

1. **Stand for Truth**: The Rider on the White Horse calls us to live with integrity and courage, challenging the forces of deception in our own lives.
2. **Use Words Wisely**: The sword of truth reminds us of the power of words to inspire, heal, and transform. How are you using your voice to bring light into the world?

3. **Confront Injustice**: The Fall of the Beast and the False Prophet challenges us to dismantle systems of harm and to build communities rooted in justice and compassion.
4. **Trust in Renewal**: The binding of Satan assures us that chaos and destruction are not permanent. How can you participate in the work of restoration and renewal in your own life?

THE CALL TO PARTICIPATE

The final battle is not just a moment in Revelation; it is a call to action for all of us. It challenges us to confront the forces of fear, deception, and corruption in our own lives and to stand firm in the pursuit of truth, justice, and grace. It reminds us that while the struggle between good and evil is ongoing, the ultimate victory has already been secured.

As we reflect on this powerful imagery, let us carry its lessons into our daily lives. Let us live with courage, speak with clarity, and act with love, trusting that the light of grace will always prevail over the shadows of fear.

CHAPTER TEN

THE NEW HEAVEN AND NEW EARTH—A VISION OF ULTIMATE RENEWAL

As Revelation reaches its conclusion, we are presented with the most breathtaking and hopeful vision of all: the creation of a new heaven and a new earth. This imagery is not just a promise of restoration but a profound invitation to imagine a world fully aligned with divine love and purpose. The New Heaven and New Earth symbolize the fulfillment of God's plan, a reality where all things are made new, and harmony is fully restored.

This chapter explores the meaning and implications of this vision, inviting readers to reflect on how it applies to their own lives and to humanity's collective journey. It is a vision of hope and grace that challenges us to participate in the work of renewal, trusting in the promise of divine transformation.

THE PASSING OF THE OLD

"Then I saw a new heaven and a new earth, for the first heaven and the first earth had passed away, and there was no longer any sea." (Revelation 21:1)

The vision begins with the passing of the old heaven and earth, symbolizing the end of systems and realities that are no longer aligned with divine purpose. The absence of the sea—a symbol of chaos and separation in biblical imagery—emphasizes the arrival of perfect peace and unity.

For modern readers, this imagery challenges us to reflect on what we need to release in our own lives. What old patterns, systems, or beliefs are no longer serving us or contributing to the greater good? The passing of the old is not about loss but about making space for the new.

THE HOLY CITY: THE NEW JERUSALEM

"I saw the Holy City, the new Jerusalem, coming down out of heaven from God, prepared as a bride beautifully dressed for her husband." (Revelation 21:2)

The New Jerusalem is the centerpiece of this vision, a city that represents the ultimate union between God and humanity. Its beauty and perfection reflect the fulfillment of divine promises, a world where love, justice, and grace reign supreme.

Unlike the earthly Jerusalem, which has been marked by conflict and division, the New Jerusalem is a city of inclusion and peace. Its open gates and radiant light symbolize a community where everyone is welcome, where barriers are broken down, and where harmony prevails. For modern readers, the New Jerusalem invites us to imagine and work toward a world that reflects these value.

GOD DWELLING AMONG HUMANITY

"Look! God's dwelling place is now among the people, and he will dwell with them. They will be his people, and God himself will be with them and be their God." (Revelation 21:3)

One of the most profound aspects of this vision is the promise of God's presence. The New Heaven and New Earth are not just places of perfection; they are places of intimate connection with the divine. The separation between God and humanity is fully overcome, and divine love permeates every aspect of existence.

For modern readers, this promise reminds us that the ultimate goal of faith is not escape but a relationship. It challenges us to cultivate a sense of divine presence in our daily lives, to see every moment as an opportunity to connect with grace, and to live in alignment with divine purpose.

THE END OF SUFFEING

"He will wipe every tear from their eyes. There will be no more death or mourning or crying or pain, for the old order of things has passed away." (Revelation 21:4)

The New Heaven and New Earth are defined by the absence of suffering. This imagery speaks to the deep human longing for healing, peace, and wholeness. It is a vision of a world where pain and loss are no more, replaced by joy and fulfillment.

For those who carry burdens of grief, trauma, or fear, this promise offers profound hope. It reminds us that no matter how great our struggles are, they are not the end of the story. The vision of the New Heaven and New Earth assures us that renewal is always possible and that divine love has the power to heal even the deepest wounds.

THE RADIANCE OF THE NEW JERUSALEM

"The city does not need the sun or the moon to shine on it, for the glory of God gives it light, and the Lamb is its lamp."(Revelation 21:23)

The New Jerusalem is a city of light, illuminated not by earthly sources but by the presence of God and the Lamb. This radiance symbolizes the clarity, truth, and grace that define the new reality. There is no darkness in this city, no hidden corners of fear or deception.

For modern readers, this vision challenges us to bring light into our lives and communities. It invites us to live transparently, seek truth, and reflect divine love in all we do. The radiance of the New Jerusalem reminds us that light always overcomes darkness and that we are called to be bearers of that light.

THE RIVER OF LIFE AND THE TREE OF LIFE

"Then the angel showed me the river of the water of life, as clear as crystal, flowing from the throne of God and of the Lamb down the

middle of the great street of the city. On each side of the river stood the tree of life." (Revelation 22:1–2)

The vision concludes with the River of Life and the Tree of Life, symbols of abundance, healing, and eternal renewal. The river flows directly from the throne of God, emphasizing its divine source, while the tree bears fruit in every season, and its leaves bring healing to the nations.

These images speak to the interconnectedness of creation and the divine. They remind us that renewal is not just an individual process but a communal one, rooted in grace and shared among all. The River and Tree of Life invite us to reflect on how we can nurture renewal in our own lives and in the world around us.

A UNIVERSAL INVITATION

"The Spirit and the bride say, 'Come!' And let the one who hears say, 'Come!' Let the one who is thirsty come, and let the one who wishes take the free gift of the water of life." (Revelation 22:17)

The vision of the New Heaven and New Earth concludes with an invitation, extended to all who seek renewal and grace. This invitation reflects the inclusive nature of divine love, reminding us that the promise of Revelation is for everyone.

For modern readers, this invitation challenges us to live with openness and generosity, extend grace to others, and participate in the work of renewal. It reminds us that we are all called to drink from the River of Life and share its blessings with the world.

LESSONS FROM THE NEW HEAVEN AND NEW EARTH

1. **Release the Old**: The passing of the old heaven and earth reminds us to let go of what no longer serves us, creating space for renewal.
2. **Cultivate Connection**: The vision of God dwelling among humanity challenges us to nurture our relationship with the divine and with one another.

3. **Bring Light into the World**: The radiance of the New Jerusalem inspires us to live transparently and truthfully, reflecting divine love in all we do.
4. **Participating in Renewal**: The River and Tree of Life reminds us that renewal is a communal process. How can you contribute to healing and growth in your own life and in the world?

THE CALL TO HOPE

The vision of the New Heaven and New Earth is the culmination of Revelation's message: that no matter how great our struggles are, renewal is always possible. It is a vision of a world transformed by love and grace, a world where all things are made new.

As we reflect on this vision, let us carry its lessons into our lives. Let us live with hope, courage, and purpose, trusting in the promise of divine renewal and working to create a world that reflects the light of the New Jerusalem.

CHAPTER ELEVEN

THE ETERNAL REIGN OF GOD—THE ALPHA AND THE OMEGA

As the Book of Revelation reaches its triumphant conclusion, we are presented with the ultimate vision of God's eternal reign. This moment is the culmination of all that has come before—a declaration of the divine plan fulfilled and the promise of eternity realized. The imagery of the Alpha and the Omega, the beginning and the end, emphasizes God's sovereignty over all creation and the timeless nature of divine love and grace.

This chapter is not merely a conclusion; it is an affirmation. It invites us to reflect on the eternal nature of God's presence in our lives and in the world. It is a call to live with trust and hope, knowing that the divine story is one of renewal, justice, and infinite love.

THE ALPHA AND THE OMEGA

"I am the Alpha and the Omega, the First and the Last, the Beginning and the End." (Revelation 22:13)

These powerful words encapsulate the essence of Revelation's message: that God is eternal, encompassing all of time and creation. The Alpha and Omega, the first and last letters of the Greek alphabet, symbolize God's presence at every stage of existence. There is no beginning or end without God, and every moment is held within divine purpose.

For modern readers, this declaration challenges us to see our lives within the broader arc of divine love. It reminds us that no matter where we are in our journey—whether at a beginning, an end, or somewhere in between—we are always encompassed by grace.

THE RIVER OF LIFE FLOWS FOREVER

"Then the angel showed me the river of the water of life, as clear as crystal, flowing from the throne of God and of the Lamb." (Revelation 22:1)

The eternal reign of God is marked by abundance, symbolized by the River of Life that flows from the throne. This imagery speaks to the continuous outpouring of divine grace and renewal, a reminder that God's blessings are never-ending.

In our own lives, the River of Life invites us to remain open to the flow of grace, trusting that even in times of drought or struggle, the waters of renewal are always present. It challenges us to share this grace with others, becoming conduits of divine love and healing.

NO MORE NIGHT

"There will be no more night. They will not need the light of a lamp or the light of the sun, for the Lord God will give them light. And they will reign forever and ever." (Revelation 22:5)

The absence of night in the eternal city symbolizes the end of fear, uncertainty, and separation. In the presence of God's eternal light, there is no darkness, no hidden corners of doubt or despair. This is a vision of perfect clarity and peace, where God's presence illuminates all things.

For modern readers, this imagery encourages us to live in the light and to seek truth and clarity in all we do. It reminds us that even in the darkest moments of our lives, the light of divine love is always present, guiding us toward renewal and hope.

THE INVITATION TO ALL

"The Spirit and the bride say, 'Come!' And let the one who hears say, 'Come!' Let the one who is thirsty come, and let the one who wishes take the free gift of the water of life." (Revelation 22:17)

The eternal reign of God is marked by inclusivity. The invitation to drink from the water of life is extended to all who seek it, reflecting the boundless nature of divine love. This universal call reminds us that grace is not reserved for a select few but is offered freely to everyone.

This invitation challenges us to live with openness and generosity, to welcome others into the flow of grace, and to recognize the divine image in all people. It is a call to build communities that reflect the inclusivity of God's eternal kingdom.

BEHOLD, I AM COMING SOON

"Look, I am coming soon! My reward is with me, and I will give to each person according to what they have done."(Revelation 22:12)

The promise of Christ's return is a central theme of Revelation's conclusion. It is not a threat but an assurance that divine justice and renewal are always on the horizon. The message is one of accountability, inviting us to live with intention and purpose, knowing that our actions have meaning and impact.

For modern readers, this promise challenges us to live each day as a reflection of divine love. It reminds us that our choices matter, that every act of kindness, every moment of integrity, contributes to the unfolding of God's plan.

THE ETERNAL REIGN AS A CALL TO ACTION

The vision of God's eternal reign is not just a promise for the future; it is a call to live in alignment with divine values here and now. It challenges us to:

- **Embrace Grace**: Trust in the boundless love of God and let it guide your actions and relationships.
- **Seek the Light**: Live with transparency, honesty, and a commitment to truth.
- **Welcome Others**: Extend the invitation of grace to all, building communities of inclusion and compassion.
- **Live with Purpose**: Recognize the significance of your actions and strive to reflect divine love in all you do.

LESSONS FROM THE ETERNAL REIGN

1. **Trust in Divine Presence**: The Alpha and Omega remind us that God is with us at every moment, from beginning to end. How can you cultivate a deeper awareness of divine presence in your life?
2. **Share the Flow of Grace**: The River of Life flows abundantly, inviting us to receive and share its blessings. How can you be a source of renewal and hope for others?
3. **Reflect the Light**: The absence of night challenges us to live with clarity and courage, bringing light into the world. What steps can you take to align your life with truth and love?
4. **Welcome the Invitation**: The call to "Come" is extended to all. How can you embody this inclusivity, welcoming others into the flow of grace and renewal?

THE PROMISE FULFILLED

The eternal reign of God is the fulfillment of all Revelation's promises—a world renewed, a creation restored, and a humanity reconciled with the divine. It is a vision of infinite love and grace, a reminder that no matter how great the struggles we face, the story of humanity is ultimately a story of hope.

As we reflect on this vision, let us carry its lessons into our lives. Let us live with trust, courage, and purpose, knowing that the Alpha and the Omega, the beginning and the end, are always present, guiding us toward renewal and grace.

THE SEVEN CHURCHES: LESSONS FOR TODAY

The letters to the seven churches in Revelation are deeply personal and profoundly instructive. Written to early Christian communities in Asia Minor, they address both the strengths and struggles of these congregations, offering praise, rebuke, and encouragement. More than historical documents, these letters remain relevant today, providing insights into the challenges of faith, the dangers of complacency, and the enduring call to perseverance and renewal.

Each church represents a facet of spiritual and communal life. In Ephesus, the community was commended for its diligence and endurance but chastised for losing its first love. This warning speaks to the danger of mechanical devotion, where faith becomes routine rather than heartfelt. In Smyrna, the church was praised for its steadfastness in the face of persecution, a reminder of the courage required to hold onto faith when external pressures are immense. Pergamum, situated in a city known for its moral and spiritual compromise, was urged to resist blending with cultural norms that conflicted with divine truth.

Thyatira, known for its love and service, faced the challenge of tolerating harmful influences, reflecting the need to balance compassion with accountability. Sardis was a church with a reputation for life but was called out for spiritual death, illustrating the perils of complacency. Philadelphia was praised for its faithfulness and the open door set before it, symbolizing opportunities for growth and witness. Lastly, Laodicea, the lukewarm church, was neither hot nor cold, embodying spiritual indifference that required a call to renewal.

These messages are timeless. Today, they challenge us to evaluate our own faith and community dynamics. Have we lost our passion for what matters most? Are we holding firm in the face of cultural or personal compromise? Are we vigilant against the creeping influence of apathy? Revelation's letters to the churches urge us to reflect deeply and act decisively, reminding us that renewal is always possible and that faithfulness yields eternal rewards.

THE ROLE OF ANGELS IN REVELATION

The angels in Revelation are as integral to the narrative as the visions themselves. They appear as messengers, protectors, warriors, and guides, embodying the connection between the divine and the earthly. They do not act independently but carry out the will of God, emphasizing the active involvement of the divine in the world and the unfolding of Revelation's events.

The angels of the seven churches serve as intermediaries, delivering God's words to the congregations. Their presence reminds us that divine guidance is always near, even in times of uncertainty or struggle. They are not merely celestial beings but symbols of the ways God communicates with humanity, whether through scripture, intuition, or the actions of others.

As warriors, angels engage in the cosmic battle against darkness. The image of Michael and his heavenly host triumphing over the Dragon is both a reassurance and a call to courage. It reflects the struggle between good and evil not just on a cosmic scale but within the human heart. The angels' victory reminds us of the ultimate triumph of light and love, encouraging us to stand firm in our own battles.

Angels also serve as guides, leading John through his visions and explaining the mysteries he encounters. Their role as interpreters mirrors the way divine wisdom often comes to us—through insight, study, and reflection. They challenge us to seek understanding, to look beyond the surface, and to embrace the deeper truths of faith.

Revelation's portrayal of angels invites us to see the unseen, to recognize the presence of grace in our lives, and to trust in the divine order even when chaos seems to reign. It is a reminder that we are never alone and that God's messengers, in whatever form they take, are always near.

REVELATION AND ENVIRONMENTAL STEWARDSHIP

The natural imagery in Revelation—the River of Life, the Tree of Life, the plagues, and the renewal of the earth—offers a profound commentary on humanity's relationship with creation. The vision of the New Jerusalem, with its harmonious integration of the natural and the divine, serves as an aspirational model for how we might live in balance with the Earth.

The River of Life flows from the throne of God, its clarity and purity symbolizing the divine source of all life. The Tree of Life, bearing fruit in every season and offering leaves for healing, reflects abundance, interconnectedness, and renewal. These images are not only spiritual symbols but also a call to protect the natural world, recognizing its sacredness and its role in sustaining life.

In contrast, the ecological disasters described in Revelation—the poisoned waters, scorched earth, and dying seas—are stark reminders of the consequences of neglecting creation. These plagues are not punishments but reflections of the harm humanity inflicts when greed and exploitation take precedence over stewardship.

Revelation challenges us to view the environment not as a resource to be exploited but as a gift to be cherished and nurtured. The vision of the New Jerusalem calls for a world where humanity lives in harmony with nature, a world where creation is respected and protected.

In our time, this message is more urgent than ever. Climate change, deforestation, and pollution threaten the balance of life on Earth. Revelation invites us to see these issues not just as scientific or political challenges but as spiritual ones. It calls us to act with wisdom and care, to restore what has been damaged, and to create a future where the Earth can thrive.

THE GLOBAL MESSAGE OF REVELATION

Revelation is a deeply universal text, transcending its historical context to speak to the shared human experience. Its vision of the New Jerusalem, where people from every nation and tribe gather in unity, is a powerful affirmation of inclusivity and diversity. It reminds us that the promise of renewal is for all people, regardless of background, culture, or creed.

The great multitude standing before the throne, clothed in white robes, is a vision of global harmony. It celebrates the richness of humanity's diversity while emphasizing the shared values of love, grace, and justice. This imagery challenges us to break down the barriers that divide us—whether they are cultural, political, or spiritual—and to work toward a world where unity and peace prevail.

Revelation's global message also addresses the systemic issues that perpetuate inequality and harm. The fall of Babylon, representing greed and corruption, is a call to confront the structures that oppress and exploit. The vision of the New Jerusalem, with its open gates and healing leaves, is an invitation to create systems that uplift and empower.

This message is profoundly relevant in today's interconnected world. Revelation calls us to recognize our shared humanity and to act with compassion and justice on a global scale. It challenges us to advocate for the marginalized, to work for peace, and to build bridges rather than walls.

At its core, Revelation's global message is one of hope. It assures us that no matter how great the challenges we face, a better world is possible—a world where love reigns, differences are celebrated, and the light of grace shines on all.

THE THRONE ROOM OF HEAVEN

The vision of the throne room in Revelation 4–5 is a cornerstone of the book, offering a glimpse into the majesty and sovereignty of God. John, transported in the Spirit, describes a scene of unparalleled beauty and awe: a throne surrounded by a rainbow that gleams like an emerald, flashes of lightning and peals of thunder emanating from its presence, and twenty-four elders casting their crowns before the One who sits upon it. At the center of this vision is not only a display of divine power but also a profound reminder of divine grace and purpose.

The Lamb, standing as though slain, takes center stage. This juxtaposition of sacrifice and victory encapsulates the heart of Revelation's message. The Lamb is worthy to open the scroll, a symbol of divine will and the unfolding of history. This moment is not just about the Lamb's authority but about the redemption and renewal offered through divine love. The elders and creatures erupt in worship, declaring the Lamb's worthiness to receive power, wealth, wisdom, strength, honor, glory, and blessings.

For modern readers, this scene challenges us to reimagine our understanding of power. The throne room portrays power not as dominance but as the ability to bring about transformation through humility and sacrifice. It invites us to reflect on what we place at the center of our lives—our own thrones of control or the divine throne of grace. Worship in the throne room is not passive adoration; it is an active acknowledgment of divine truth and a call to align our lives with that truth.

THE GREAT MULTITUDE

Revelation 7:9–17 introduces us to a vision of inclusivity and unity that transcends time and place. John describes a vast crowd, too numerous to count, made up of people from every nation, tribe, people, and language. They stand before the throne of God and the Lamb, clothed in white robes and holding palm branches, symbols of victory and peace.

This scene powerfully reminds us that Revelation's promise of renewal is for all. It challenges any notion of exclusivity, celebrating humanity's diversity while emphasizing the unity found in divine grace. These individuals have "come out of the great tribulation," their robes washed in the blood of the Lamb, signifying not just suffering but perseverance and redemption.

The great multitude also speaks to the endurance of faith. In a world often marked by division and conflict, this vision inspires hope for a future where unity prevails. For modern readers, it calls us to embrace diversity, recognize the shared humanity in all people, and work toward communities that reflect the harmony of this heavenly gathering.

THE TWO WITNESSES

The story of the two witnesses in Revelation 11 is rich with symbolism and intrigue. These figures, empowered to prophesy for 1,260 days, are described as olive trees and lampstands, representing their connection to divine power and their role as bearers of light. They stand as a testament to truth, proclaiming the message of God in the face of opposition.

The witnesses are a powerful example of resilience. Despite being attacked and even killed, they are resurrected and ascend to heaven, symbolizing the triumph of truth over falsehood and the ultimate vindication of faith. Their story reminds us that standing for what is right often comes with challenges but that perseverance leads to eternal reward.

In modern life, the two witnesses challenge us to be voices of truth and justice, even in the face of adversity. They remind us that our actions, no matter how small, contribute to the larger narrative of grace and renewal.

THE BEAST AND THE MARK OF THE BEAST

The Beast and its mark in Revelation 13 have long been subjects of speculation and fear. Yet, when viewed through the lens of symbolism, they reveal profound truths about the tension between allegiance to God and allegiance to corrupt systems.

The Beast rising from the sea represents worldly powers that oppose divine truth, while the second Beast promotes false worship. The mark of the Beast, placed on the forehead or hand, signifies a willful alignment with these forces. This imagery challenges readers to reflect on the systems they support and the values they embody.

For modern readers, the mark of the Beast is a call to discernment. It invites us to examine our choices and the ways they reflect our allegiance—to divine love or to destructive forces of greed, power, and fear. It reminds us that true freedom comes not from conforming to the world but from aligning with divine purpose.

THE FALL OF SATAN

The dramatic account of Satan's fall in Revelation 12:7–12 portrays the cosmic battle between good and evil. Michael and his angels defeat the Dragon, casting it out of heaven. This victory symbolizes the triumph of divine truth over deception and chaos.

The fall of Satan is not just a cosmic event but a reflection of the ongoing struggle within each of us. It reminds us of the power of faith and the assurance that light will always overcome darkness. For modern readers, this passage is a call to resist the forces of fear and division, trusting in the ultimate victory of grace.

THE MARRIAGE OF THE LAMB

The wedding supper of the Lamb in Revelation 19:6–9 is a moment of joy and fulfillment. This union between Christ and His people symbolizes the ultimate restoration of the relationship between humanity and the divine.

The imagery of a wedding speaks to intimacy, celebration, and unity. It reminds us that faith is not about obligation but about connection—a deep, personal relationship with the Creator. For modern readers, the marriage of the Lamb inspires us to nurture our spiritual lives and to celebrate the beauty of divine love.

THE FINAL JUDGMENT

Revelation 20:11–15 presents the Great White Throne's judgment, a scene often associated with fear. Yet, when viewed through the lens of compassion, it becomes a moment of accountability and healing. Each person is judged according to their deeds, but the focus is on the Book of Life, a record of transformation and renewal.

For modern readers, the final judgment is not a threat but an invitation to live with purpose. It challenges us to reflect on our choices and to align ourselves with values of love, justice, and truth. It reminds us that grace is always available and that transformation is possible.

THE RIVER OF LIFE AND THE TREE OF LIFE

The closing chapters of Revelation introduce the River of Life and the Tree of Life, symbols of healing, renewal, and abundance. These elements emphasize the interconnectedness of creation and the divine, inviting us to see the sacred in the natural world.

For modern readers, this imagery is a call to stewardship. It reminds us of our responsibility to care for the Earth and to work toward a future where all can thrive in harmony with creation.

THE SEVEN SPIRITS OF GOD

The Seven Spirits of God, mentioned throughout Revelation, symbolize the fullness of divine presence. They represent wisdom, understanding, counsel, might, knowledge, piety, and reverence—qualities that guide and empower humanity.

These spirits remind us that God's presence is not distant but active and accessible. For modern readers, they offer a framework for spiritual growth and a reminder of the divine support available in every moment.

THE SONGS OF REVELATION

The songs in Revelation are declarations of worship, joy, and hope. They punctuate the narrative, offering moments of celebration and reflection. These songs remind us of the power of gratitude and the importance of lifting our voices in praise.

For modern readers, the songs of Revelation invite us to cultivate a spirit of worship in our daily lives. They challenge us to find joy in the midst of struggle and to celebrate the beauty of grace.

THE SOUND OF REVELATION: THE TRANSFORMATIVE POWER OF DIVINE HARMONY

The Book of Revelation is not only a visual masterpiece but also an auditory symphony, rich with sounds that convey the drama, majesty, and profound truths of its message. From the thunderous voice of God to the songs of the heavenly hosts, Revelation uses sound to draw readers into its cosmic narrative, emphasizing both its urgency and its beauty. To truly grasp the depth of Revelation, we must listen as much as we look, allowing its soundscape to resonate within our souls.

THE VOICE OF GOD: THUNDER AND INTIMACY

Revelation frequently describes God's voice as *"like the sound of many waters"* (Revelation 1:15) or *"like thunder"* (Revelation 14:2). These descriptions evoke both the majesty and the mystery of the divine. The sound of many waters suggests a vast, overwhelming presence, reminding us of the power of the Creator. Thunder, on the other hand, is sudden and attention-grabbing, a sound that commands awe and reverence.

Yet, amidst these grand auditory symbols, God's voice also speaks with clarity and intimacy, particularly when addressing the seven churches. This duality of sound—awe-inspiring and deeply personal—reflects the relationship between humanity and the divine. It reminds us that while God is transcendent, God is also near, speaking directly to our hearts.

For modern readers, the voice of God in Revelation invites us to listen deeply, to tune in to the sacred amidst the noise of daily life. It challenges us to recognize the ways God speaks to us, whether through moments of thunderous realization or the gentle whispers of intuition and grace.

THE TRUMPETS: CALLS TO AWAKENING

The sound of trumpets in Revelation is both alarming and profound. Each of the seven trumpets heralds a significant event, their blasts cutting through complacency and calling humanity to reflection and action. Trumpets have long been associated with divine intervention, from the walls of Jericho to the return of Christ. In Revelation, they serve as a wake-up call, urging us to confront the realities of our world and our lives.

The trumpets' urgency reflects the need for spiritual awakening. They challenge us to examine our priorities, to address the injustices and failings within and around us, and to realign ourselves with divine purpose. Their sound is not meant to instill fear but to inspire transformation.

For modern readers, the trumpets remind us of the importance of being alert and responsive to the spiritual and moral challenges of our time. They call us to act with integrity and courage, trusting that even the most unsettling sounds can lead to renewal.

THE SONGS OF HEAVEN: WORSHIP AND UNITY

Revelation is filled with songs, sung by angels, elders, and the great multitude before the throne of God. These songs are expressions of worship, joy, and unity, celebrating the victory of the Lamb and the fulfillment of divine promises. They contrast the chaos and conflict of the earthly realm with the harmony and peace of the heavenly realm.

The songs of Revelation are not merely decorative; they are transformative. They invite us to participate in the act of worship, to lift our voices in gratitude and praise, and to join in the collective celebration of grace and renewal. They remind us that sound has the power to unify, to heal, and to uplift.

For modern readers, the songs of heaven challenge us to cultivate a spirit of worship in our daily lives. Whether through music, prayer, or acts of kindness, we are called to create harmony in our communities and to reflect the beauty of divine love.

THE SILENCE IN HEAVEN: REVERENCE AND REFLECTION

One of the most striking auditory moments in Revelation is the silence in heaven that follows the opening of the seventh seal (Revelation 8:1). This silence, lasting "about half an hour," is a powerful pause in the midst of Revelation's dramatic narrative. It is a moment of reverence, reflection, and anticipation.

Silence in Revelation is not emptiness; it is fullness. It is the space where the divine presence is most deeply felt, where words and sounds fall away, and only awe remains. This silence invites us to stop, to listen, and to prepare our hearts for what is to come.

For modern readers, the silence in heaven reminds them of the importance of stillness. In a world filled with constant noise, silence becomes a sacred act, a way to connect with the divine and to center ourselves in the midst of life's chaos.

THE SOUND OF JUDGMENT AND RENEWAL

Revelation is not shy about using sound to depict judgment and renewal. The thunder, earthquakes, and roaring waters that accompany the plagues and the fall of Babylon symbolize the upheaval necessary for transformation. These sounds are not merely destructive; they are purifying, clearing the way for the New Jerusalem.

At the same time, the gentle sounds of the River of Life and the songs of the redeemed remind us of the peace and beauty that follow renewal. Revelation's soundscape moves from discord to harmony, reflecting humanity's journey from brokenness to wholeness.

For modern readers, these sounds challenge us to embrace the cycles of judgment and renewal in our own lives. They remind us that even the loudest disruptions can lead to the quiet peace of transformation.

THE UNIVERSAL INVITATION: "COME"

One of the most profound auditory moments in Revelation is the invitation extended to all: *"The Spirit and the bride say, 'Come!' And let the one who hears say, 'Come!'"* (Revelation 22:17). This simple yet powerful word is a call to grace, inclusion, and participation in the divine story.

The invitation to "Come" is both personal and communal. It is an open call to drink from the water of life, to find renewal, and to join in the celebration of the New Jerusalem. Its sound echoes through the pages of Revelation, reminding us that we are all welcomed into the fold of grace.

For modern readers, this invitation is a call to listen and respond. It challenges us to extend the same grace to others, to create spaces of welcome and inclusion, and to live in harmony with the divine song.

REVELATION'S SOUNDTRACK FOR LIFE

The soundscape of Revelation is as much a part of its message as its imagery. It calls us to awaken, to reflect, to worship, and to act. It reminds us that sound has the power to shape our hearts, to inspire our actions, and to connect us with the divine.

As we journey through Revelation, may we not only see its visions but hear its music. May we listen to the thunderous voice of God, the urgent call of the trumpets, the joyous songs of heaven, and the reverent silence of the seventh seal. And may these sounds guide us toward lives of grace, harmony, and renewal.

THE SPECIAL GRACE OF REVELATION

A GIFT FOR READERS AND SEEKERS

The Book of Revelation begins with a profound promise: *"Blessed is the one who reads aloud the words of this prophecy and blessed are those who hear it and take to heart what is written in it, because the time is near"* (Revelation 1:3). This declaration sets Revelation apart as a text imbued with a unique grace—a grace extended to those who engage with it, whether through reading, hearing, or internalizing its message.

This grace is not conditional upon perfect understanding or mastery of its complexities. Rather, it is a gift that flows from the act of seeking—the willingness to explore its mysteries, grapple with its imagery, and open one's heart to its truths. Revelation's grace lies in its ability to transform, awaken, and guide those who approach it with sincerity and faith.

THE GRACE OF ENGAGEMENT

Reading Revelation is itself an act of faith. The vivid symbols, dramatic visions, and layered meanings can feel overwhelming or even intimidating. Yet, for those who persist, Revelation offers profound rewards. Its grace is not found in the answers it provides, but in the questions, it invites us to ask. Who are we in the cosmic story of light and darkness? How do we respond to the call to overcome? What role do we play in the unfolding vision of the New Jerusalem?

This grace is participatory. It meets us where we are, offering wisdom and insight that resonate with our unique circumstances. For some, it may bring comfort in times of struggle. For others, it may ignite a call to action or inspire a deeper connection to the divine. Whatever the outcome, the very act of engaging with Revelation aligns us with its blessing.

THE GRACE OF UNDERSTANDING

Understanding Revelation requires more than intellectual effort; it requires spiritual openness. Its grace is revealed not in decoding every symbol but in embracing its overarching themes—hope in the midst of chaos, the triumph of love over fear, and the promise of renewal for all creation. This understanding is less about knowledge and more about transformation. It is a grace that softens hearts, sharpens vision, and deepens faith.

When we approach Revelation with humility, we allow its truths to take root within us. Its grace becomes a mirror, reflecting not only the divine story but also our own journey. We begin to see ourselves in its pages—striving, overcoming, and ultimately renewed by grace. This understanding is a gift, one that draws us closer to the divine and to our true selves.

THE GRACE WITHIN YOU

The grace of Revelation is not separate from the grace already present within you. It is a divine spark that awakens something dormant—a deeper awareness of your connection to God, to others, and to the unfolding story of creation. As you read and reflect on Revelation, this grace grows, guiding you toward greater compassion, courage, and clarity.

This grace is personal yet universal. It reminds you that you are part of a larger narrative, one that spans time and space, yet it also speaks directly to your heart. It is the grace that calls you to overcome fear, to trust in the promise of renewal, and to live with purpose and love.

A GRACE THAT TRANSFORMS

Revelation's grace is not static; it is dynamic and transformative. It moves us from confusion to clarity, from fear to hope, from isolation to connection. It challenges us to see beyond the surface of our lives and to align ourselves with the divine vision of renewal and unity.

This grace also extends outward. As we receive it, we are called to share it—through acts of kindness, words of encouragement, and the ways we build communities of light and love. Revelation's grace is a gift meant to multiply, touching not only the reader but also the world around them.

LIVING IN REVELATION'S GRACE

To read Revelation is to step into a sacred space, one where divine truth and human experience meet. It is to embrace a grace that illuminates, challenges, and transforms. This grace does not demand perfection; it asks only for a willing heart and an open mind.

As you journey through Revelation, let its grace guide you. Let it deepen your understanding, strengthen your resolve, and inspire your actions. Trust that this grace is with you, not only as you read but as you live—shaping your path, renewing your spirit, and leading you toward the light of the New Jerusalem.

REVELATION'S MESSAGE ON COMING TOGETHER IN THE END TIMES

The Book of Revelation presents a profound vision of unity and reconciliation as a central theme of the end times. While much of the book depicts cosmic struggles, judgments, and upheavals, its ultimate goal is not destruction but renewal and the gathering of humanity into a harmonious, redeemed existence. Revelation's message about coming together emphasizes the triumph of love over division, the inclusion of all peoples, and the establishment of a world rooted in justice, peace, and divine presence.

THE GREAT MULTITUDE: A VISION OF UNITY

One of the most striking images in Revelation is the vision of the great multitude in Revelation 7:9–10. John describes *"a great multitude that no one could count, from every nation, tribe, people, and language, standing before the throne and before the Lamb. They were wearing white robes and were holding palm branches in their hands."*

This gathering represents humanity in its diversity, united in worship and redemption. The multitude's white robes signify purity and victory, while the palm branches echo symbols of peace and celebration. This scene challenges earthly divisions—cultural, racial, national, and linguistic—affirming that in God's kingdom, all are welcome.

For the modern reader, this vision is a powerful call to inclusivity. It reminds us that coming together is not about erasing differences but about celebrating them as part of a divine mosaic. It challenges us to build communities that reflect this heavenly unity, embracing diversity while finding a common purpose in love and grace.

THE OPEN GATES OF THE NEW JERUSALEM

In Revelation 21:25–27, the New Jerusalem is described as a city with gates that are never closed. *"Its gates will never be shut by day—and there will be no night there. The glory and honor of the nations will be brought into it."* This image of open gates symbolizes perpetual welcome, a place where all are invited to enter and participate in the divine renewal.

The nations bringing their glory into the city underscores the idea that each culture and people have something unique and valuable to contribute to the divine vision. The New Jerusalem is not a monolithic society but a gathering of the world's richness, united under the light of God.

This inclusivity contrasts sharply with the divisions and exclusions often found in human systems. Revelation's open gates remind us that true unity is rooted in grace and that the barriers we create—whether physical, social, or spiritual—must give way to a higher vision of togetherness.

THE HEALING OF THE NATIONS

Revelation 22:1–2 describes the River of Life flowing from the throne of God and the Lamb, with the Tree of Life on either side of the river. The tree's leaves are *"for the healing of the nations."*

This image speaks directly to humanity's restoration and reconciliation. Healing is not limited to individuals but extends to entire nations, addressing the wounds caused by war, injustice, and division. The Tree of Life, bearing fruit in every season, signifies abundance and sufficiency for all—a stark contrast to the scarcity and competition that often divide people.

In today's context, this vision invites us to participate in healing. It challenges us to work toward reconciliation, to address systemic inequalities, and to create environments where all people can thrive.

The healing of the nations is not a passive promise but an active call to embody the values of love, justice, and peace.

THE CALL TO UNITY AMIDST STRUGGLE

Revelation acknowledges the world's struggles and divisions. The imagery of the Beast, Babylon, and the Dragon reflects the forces of corruption, greed, and fear that separate humanity. Yet, even in the midst of this conflict, Revelation continually points toward unity as the ultimate goal.

The repeated call to "overcome" in Revelation is not just an individual mandate but a collective one. It is an invitation for humanity to rise above fear, division, and sin and to come together in faith and purpose. Revelation emphasizes that the path to unity requires perseverance, courage, and a shared commitment to the light.

THE FINAL INVITATION

The final chapter of Revelation extends a universal invitation: *"The Spirit and the bride say, 'Come!' And let the one who hears say, 'Come!' Let the one who is thirsty come, and let the one who wishes take the free gift of the water of life."*(Revelation 22:17)

This call is deeply inclusive, inviting everyone—regardless of their past or present circumstances—to partake in divine grace. It is an invitation not only to individuals but to humanity as a whole, urging us to gather at the source of life and to share in the promise of renewal.

The invitation to "Come" is also a call to action. It reminds us that unity is not achieved by waiting but by stepping forward—by extending grace to others, by building bridges, and by participating in the creation of a world that reflects the love and light of the New Jerusalem.

COMING TOGETHER IN MODERN TIMES

Revelation's vision of unity is profoundly relevant in our divided world. The conflicts and barriers that separate us—whether political, cultural, or spiritual—remind us of the work that remains to be done.

Yet, Revelation assures us that division is not the final word. Its imagery of the great multitude, the open gates, and the healing of the nations offers a blueprint for coming together.

To live out this vision, we are called to:

- Embrace Diversity: Recognize the unique contributions of every individual and culture as part of the divine tapestry.
- Work for Reconciliation: Address the wounds of division, seeking peace and understanding in our relationships and communities.
- Extend Grace: Create spaces of welcome and inclusion, reflecting the open gates of the New Jerusalem.
- Participate in Healing: Actively engage in efforts to heal systemic and personal brokenness, trusting in the power of renewal.

Revelation's message is clear: the end times are not about separation but about gathering. They are not about fear but about hope. They are not about destruction but about the promise of a world where love reigns, and all are united under the light of God's grace. This is the ultimate call of Revelation—to come together, to overcome, and to be part of the eternal story of renewal

EPILOGUE

THE ETERNAL CALL OF REVELATION

The journey through Revelation is one of profound awe and reflection, carrying us from the mysteries of divine judgment to the brilliance of eternal renewal. It begins with an invitation to witness the cosmic drama of humanity's spiritual evolution and concludes with the promise of a new heaven and a new earth—a vision of light, love, and unity that transcends all boundaries of time and place. But the true power of Revelation lies not in its dramatic imagery or apocalyptic tone but in its enduring relevance. Revelation is not merely a story of what was or what might be—it is a living, breathing guide to what can be, a call to embrace divine wisdom and walk the path of renewal.

THE CALL TO PERSONAL AND COLLECTIVE RENEWAL

The core message of Revelation is one of transformation. It reminds us that every challenge, every moment of suffering, carries within it the seeds of renewal. The trials depicted in Revelation—the seals, trumpets, and bowls—are not final acts of destruction but catalysts for growth and change. They symbolize the breaking down of what is no longer aligned with divine purpose and the emergence of a new way of being.

For us, this call to renewal is deeply personal yet profoundly collective. Each of us is invited to examine our own lives and reflect on what we need to release in order to embrace a higher way of living. Are there fears, habits, or beliefs that no longer serve us? Are there ways we can live more authentically, more compassionately, and more in tune with divine love? At the same time, Revelation calls us to think beyond ourselves and consider the collective renewal of humanity. How can we contribute to building a world that reflects the values of love, justice, and grace?

The process of renewal is not always easy. Like the imagery of Revelation itself, it can be tumultuous and unsettling. But the promise of Revelation is clear: no matter how great the challenge, the light of grace is always present, guiding us toward a brighter and more unified existence.

THE VISION OF THE NEW JERUSALEM

At the heart of Revelation's promise is the vision of the New Jerusalem, a city of light and harmony where God dwells among humanity. This city is not just a distant hope; it is a blueprint for how we are called to live in the present. The New Jerusalem symbolizes a world where barriers are broken, where every person is valued, and where love and justice reign supreme.

The beauty of the New Jerusalem lies in its inclusivity. Its gates are always open, welcoming all who seek renewal and grace. This vision challenges us to build communities that reflect this spirit of openness and unity. It calls us to embrace diversity, celebrate the unique gifts of every individual, and work together to create spaces of belonging and connection.

In our daily lives, the New Jerusalem invites us to live intentionally. How can we bring its values into our own relationships, communities, and decisions? How can we be the builders of this divine city, co-creators of a world that mirrors its light?

LIVING IN THE LIGHT

Revelation is filled with imagery of light overcoming darkness—most powerfully in the description of the New Jerusalem, where God's presence provides eternal illumination. This light represents clarity, truth, and the unwavering power of love to dispel fear and deception.

For modern readers, this symbolism serves as both a reassurance and a challenge. It reassures us that no matter how great the darkness is in our lives or in the world, the light of grace is always present, guiding us forward. At the same time, it challenges us to live as bearers of that light. How can we bring truth, kindness, and understanding into the spaces we inhabit? How can we reflect the divine light in our words, actions, and choices?

Living in the light means seeking authenticity, embracing vulnerability, and rejecting fear. It means being willing to confront the shadows within ourselves and in the world, trusting that the light of grace is strong enough to overcome them.

THE BLESSING OF REVELATION

Revelation begins with a blessing and ends with one, framing its powerful narrative within the promise of divine grace. *"Blessed is the one who reads aloud the words of this prophecy, and blessed are those who hear it and take to heart what is written in it."* (Revelation 1:3). This blessing is not reserved for scholars or theologians; it is for anyone who engages with its message with an open heart and a willingness to grow.

The blessing of Revelation is an invitation to reflect, learn, and act. It calls us to take its lessons to heart and allow them to shape our lives. It reminds us that faith is not about passive belief but about active participation in the unfolding of divine grace.

AN ETERNAL INVITATION

Revelation concludes with an invitation that echoes through eternity: *"The Spirit and the bride say, 'Come!' And let the one who hears say, 'Come!' Let the one who is thirsty come, and let the one who wishes take the free gift of the water of life."* (Revelation 22:17). This invitation is extended to all who seek renewal and connection, a testament to the boundless nature of divine love.

For modern readers, this universal call challenges us to live with openness and generosity. How can we extend grace to others, welcoming them into the flow of divine love? How can we create communities that reflect the inclusivity of this invitation? The call to "come" is not just for us to receive; it is also for us to share, to become conduits of grace and renewal in the lives of others.

CARRYING REVELATION'S MESSAGE FORWARD

The message of Revelation is timeless. It speaks not only to the struggles and hopes of the early Church but also to the challenges and aspirations of our own time. It reminds us that humanity's story is ultimately a story of hope—a journey from brokenness to renewal, from separation to unity, from darkness to light.

As we carry Revelation's message forward, we are called to embody its values in our own lives. We are called to be builders of the New Jerusalem, bearers of light, and participants in the eternal flow of grace. This is not a passive calling; it is an active, transformative process that requires courage, intention, and love.

THE PROMISE FULFILLED

Revelation assures us that no matter how great the trials we face, the promise of renewal is always within reach. It is a reminder that God's story is one of love, justice, and infinite grace. The final words of Revelation, simple yet profound, leave us with the ultimate assurance: *"Amen. Come, Lord Jesus. The grace of the Lord Jesus be with God's people. Amen."* (Revelation 22:20–21).

This is the promise of Revelation—a promise not of fear but of hope, not of destruction but of renewal. It is the assurance that all things can be made new, and that divine love will always have the final word.

CLOSING REFLECTION

As you turn the final page of this book, may the message of Revelation take root in your heart as a wellspring of hope, inspiration, and guidance. May its timeless truths resonate deeply within you, urging you to live with intention and to embrace each moment as an opportunity for growth and renewal.

Let Revelation's profound vision remind you that you are part of a story far greater than yourself—a story of light overcoming darkness, of grace triumphing over fear, and of love transforming all it touches. May it encourage you to face life's challenges with courage, knowing that every trial is an invitation to grow stronger, wiser, and more attuned to the divine presence that surrounds and sustains you.

Let its call to action inspire you to live with purpose, not only for yourself but for the world around you. May it move you to act with compassion, to be a light in the lives of others, and to contribute to the collective work of healing and renewal. Remember that even the smallest acts of kindness, forgiveness, and understanding are reflections of the New Jerusalem—a vision of unity, peace, and grace made manifest through our choices and actions.

And when the path feels uncertain, or the weight of the world feels heavy, let the promise of grace be your anchor. Trust in its transformative power, its ability to make all things new, and its unwavering presence in every moment of your journey. Revelation is not a tale of endings but a proclamation of beginnings, a reminder that renewal is always possible and that no soul is beyond the reach of divine love.

Above all, may the eternal light of the New Jerusalem guide you, even in the darkest hours. May it shine as a beacon of hope, illuminating the way toward a world shaped by love, compassion, and justice—a world where every tear is wiped away, and every heart finds its home in the embrace of grace.

Carry this vision with you, and let it transform the way you see the world, the way you love, and the way you live. Revelation is not merely a text to read; it is a journey to take, a truth to embody, and a promise to hold dear.

With this light in your heart, may you go forward inspired, renewed, and ready to be part of the story of a world transformed by love.

GLOSSARY OF SYMBOLS IN REVELATION

The Book of Revelation is a treasure trove of powerful symbols and vivid imagery, each carrying profound spiritual meaning. To help readers navigate its rich landscape, this glossary provides brief descriptions of key symbols and their significance.

The Lamb

- **Description**: A central figure in Revelation, often referred to as the Lamb that was slain.
- **Meaning**: The Lamb represents Jesus Christ, symbolizing humility, sacrifice, and divine love. The Lamb's triumph over the forces of darkness illustrates the power of grace and forgiveness.

The Dragon

- **Description**: A fiery red, seven-headed beast that wages war against the faithful.
- **Meaning**: Symbolizes chaos, fear, and the forces of evil. The Dragon embodies the challenges and opposition faced by those who align themselves with truth and love.

The Beast

- **Description**: Two beasts—one rising from the sea, the other from the earth—are described in Revelation.
- **Meaning**: Represent systems of corruption, oppression, and deception. The Beast is a warning against aligning with false power and worldly greed.

The New Jerusalem

- **Description**: A radiant, heavenly city descending from God, with streets of gold and gates of pearl.

- **Meaning**: Symbolizes the fulfillment of divine promises—a world renewed and aligned with love, justice, and peace.

The River of Life

- **Description**: A crystal-clear river flowing from the throne of God and the Lamb.
- **Meaning**: Represents divine grace, abundance, and the eternal flow of renewal and healing.

The Tree of Life

- **Description**: A tree bearing fruit in every season, with leaves for the healing of nations.
- **Meaning**: A symbol of eternal life, healing, and the interconnectedness of creation.

The Seven Seals

- **Description**: A series of divine decrees revealed as each seal of a scroll is broken.
- **Meaning**: Represent stages of spiritual reckoning and transformation, emphasizing humanity's journey toward renewal.

The Seven Trumpets

- **Description**: Trumpets sounded by angels, each heralding a significant event.
- **Meaning**: Symbols of divine intervention and awakening, calling humanity to reflect and realign with divine purpose.

The Seven Bowls

- **Description**: Bowls of wrath poured out upon the earth as part of the final reckoning.
- **Meaning**: Represent the purification of creation, clearing the way for the establishment of divine harmony.

The Alpha and the Omega

- **Description**: Titles for God, signifying the beginning and the end.
- **Meaning**: Represent God's eternal nature and sovereignty over all creation, reminding us of the divine presence at every moment.

The Mark of the Beast

- **Description**: A mark placed on the foreheads or hands of those who follow the Beast.
- **Meaning**: Represents allegiance to corrupt systems and a rejection of divine truth. A call to examine where our loyalties lie.

The Bride

- **Description**: The faithful is symbolized as the bride of Christ.
- **Meaning**: Represents the collective community of believers, called to prepare for union with the divine through love and faithfulness.

The Great Multitude

- **Description**: A vast assembly of people from every nation, standing before the throne of God.
- **Meaning**: Symbolizes the inclusivity of divine grace, a vision of unity and diversity in the New Jerusalem.

Maps of Revelation's Visions

- A Map of the New Jerusalem
    - Description: A visual representation of the city as described in Revelation 21–22.
    - Features:
        - Twelve gates, each named after a tribe of Israel.
        - Streets of gold, with the River of Life flowing through the center.
        - The Tree of Life on either side of the river.
- A Map of Patmos and the Seven Churches
    - Description: A geographical depiction of the island of Patmos, where John wrote Revelation, and the locations of the seven churches addressed in Revelation 2–3.
    - Features:
        - Patmos in the Aegean Sea.
        - Locations of Ephesus, Smyrna, Pergamum, Thyatira, Sardis, Philadelphia, and Laodicea.

ADDITIONAL NOTES

This glossary and accompanying maps are designed to deepen your understanding of Revelation's profound symbolism and themes. Use them as a guide to explore the text's richness and connect its timeless messages to your own spiritual journey.

Here's a detailed map of the New Jerusalem based on the description from Revelation.

ABOUT THE AUTHOR

Tina Ketch is a visionary author, renowned for her ability to illuminate profound spiritual truths with clarity and compassion. With over 40 published works, Tina has dedicated her life to exploring themes of transformation, renewal, and the eternal journey of the soul. Her writing draws upon her deep understanding of sacred texts, psychology, and the human experience, offering readers guidance and hope in their quest for meaning and purpose.

Tina's unique approach blends ancient wisdom with modern insights, making complex concepts accessible and relatable. In *Behold, All Things New: A Modern Interpretation of the Book of Revelation*, she brings the powerful imagery and messages of Revelation into the present day, offering a fresh perspective on its timeless truths. Her interpretation moves beyond fear-based readings, uncovering Revelation's core message of love, grace, and renewal.

As a world traveler and seeker of spiritual wisdom, Tina's work is informed by her journey through life's challenges and triumphs. She has known deep loss and profound love, experiences that have shaped her empathetic and insightful approach to writing. Tina is passionate about inspiring others to live with purpose, embrace the power of renewal, and trust in the infinite possibilities of grace.

Through her books, Tina continues to touch lives around the world, inviting readers to reflect, grow, and transform. Her mission is simple yet profound: to guide others toward the light of hope and to remind them that, no matter how great the challenges, all things can be made new.

To learn more about Tina Ketch and her work, visit her online at TinaKetch.com.

A NOTE TO THE READER

Dear Reader,

Thank you for picking up this book and stepping into the powerful and often misunderstood world of Revelation. Writing this book has been a deeply personal journey for me—a journey not just through the words of Scripture, but through my own heart, questions, and hopes. My desire is to share with you the profound beauty and timeless truths I have found in Revelation, truths that I believe are meant for all of us.

For many, the Book of Revelation has been a source of fear. Its imagery of beasts, battles, and judgment can feel overwhelming, even intimidating. I've often heard people say, "I don't understand it," or "It's too frightening to read." But as I've studied Revelation, I've come to see something different. Beneath its dramatic symbols and apocalyptic tone lies a story of grace, hope, and renewal—a story that speaks to the deepest longings of the human soul.

This book is not about predicting the future or decoding secret messages. It is about uncovering the eternal truths that Revelation holds for our lives today. It is about seeing Revelation not as a warning of doom but as an invitation to embrace divine love and live with courage and purpose. It is about recognizing that even in the darkest moments, light prevails and that no matter how great our struggles, all things can be made new.

My hope for this book is that it will bring you clarity, comfort, and inspiration. I hope it will encourage you to reflect on your own life, to see the light of grace at work in your challenges, and to embrace the promise of renewal that Revelation offers. I hope it will remind you that you are part of a story much bigger than yourself—a story of love, justice, and infinite grace.

This book is for anyone who has ever felt uncertain about Revelation, for those who have been overwhelmed by its imagery or unsure of its relevance. It is for the seeker, the questioner, the hopeful heart longing for renewal. It is my gift to you, offered with the prayer that it will guide you closer to the light of divine love and the eternal promise of grace.

Thank you for trusting me to take this journey with you. May this book speak to your heart, challenge your mind, and inspire your spirit. May you always remember that the story of Revelation is not one of endings but of new beginnings.

With love and gratitude,
Tina Ketch

A UNIVERSAL PRAYER

FOR RENEWAL AND GRACE

Divine Source of all that is,
We come before You, open and humble,
seeking renewal, peace, and understanding.
Guide us to walk the path of love, compassion, and truth,
To be lights in the darkness, bearers of hope,
and stewards of grace.

Help us release the burdens we carry,
The fears, doubts, and attachments that no longer serve us.
Fill the empty spaces within us with clarity,
purpose, and courage,
That we may live in alignment with Your eternal wisdom.

Teach us to see the divine in all things,
To honor the sacredness of creation and the interconnectedness of all life.
May we act with kindness, speak with sincerity,
And embrace each moment as an opportunity for growth and transformation.

Grant us the strength to face our challenges with faith,
The wisdom to learn from every trial,
And the grace to forgive others and ourselves,
Trusting always in the promise of renewal.

May our lives reflect the light of unity and peace,
May our communities be places of inclusion and justice,
And may our hearts be vessels of love that inspire and heal.

In this eternal moment, we offer our gratitude for the blessings seen and unseen,
For the promise that no matter the struggles,
All things can be made new.

Amen.

www.ingramcontent.com/pod-product-compliance
Lightning Source LLC
LaVergne TN
LVHW010937110826
845149LV00013B/2639

* 9 7 9 8 9 9 2 1 6 6 9 2 7 *